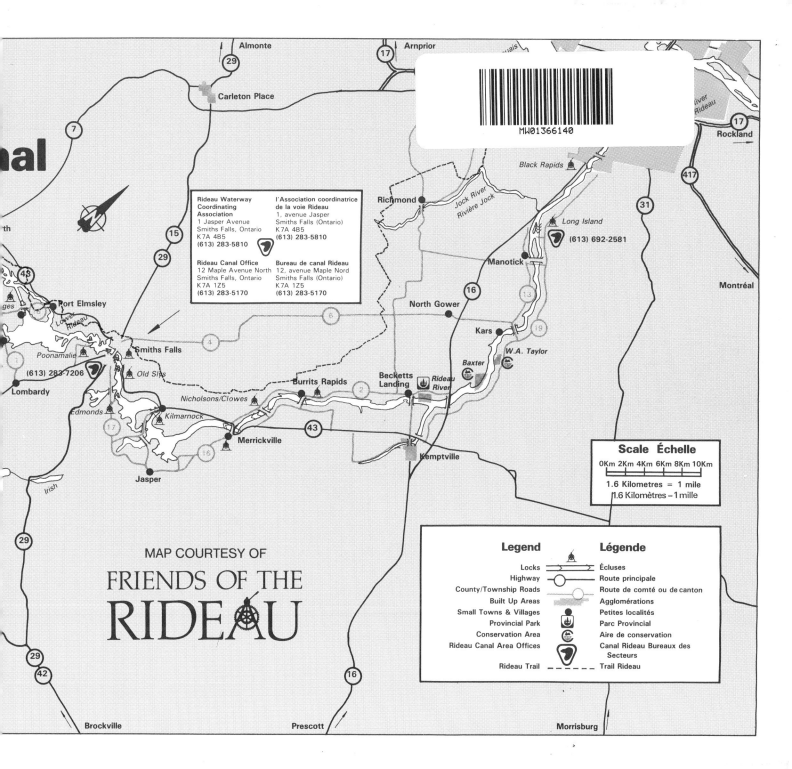

On A Sunday Afternoon
CLASSIC BOATS ON THE RIDEAU CANAL

Mr. and Mrs. Fox in a pastoral setting at Chaffey's Locks, ca. 1905.
– Neil Patterson, Pennock Collection, Canadian Parks Service

On A Sunday Afternoon

CLASSIC BOATS ON THE RIDEAU CANAL

DEWAR • DOUGLAS • TURNER • POTTER • HERWIG • PHELAN

Edited by Alec Douglas and Larry Turner

THE BOSTON MILLS PRESS

Canadian Cataloguing in Publication Data

Main entry under title:
On a Sunday afternoon : classic boats on the
Rideau Canal

ISBN 1-55046-026-9

1. Boats and boating – Ontario – Rideau Canal –
History. 2. Manotick Classic Boat Club – History.
I. Turner, Larry. II. Douglas, W.A.B. (William
Alexander Binny), 1929–

GV776.15.R4305 1989   797.1'09713'7   C89-095072-5

© Manotick Classic Boat Club, 1989

Design by John Denison, Erin
Cover design by Gill Stead, Guelph
Typeset by Speed River Graphics, Guelph
Printing by Ampersand, Guelph

Published by:
THE BOSTON MILLS PRESS
132 Main Street
Erin, Ontario
N0B 1T0

American Association
for State and Local History
Award of Merit

Winners of the
Heritage Canada
Communications Award

(519) 833-2407 (fax) 833-2195

The publisher gratefully acknowledges the financial
assistance and encouragement of The Canada
Council and the Ontario Arts Council.

CONTENTS

7   Acknowledgements
8   Introduction   *by Larry Turner*
11   Chapter 1:
     Summer's Time   *by Keith Dewar*
31   Chapter 2:
     The Long Reach   *by Alec Douglas*
45   Chapter 3:
     Rideau Boating: A Special Tradition   *by Larry Turner*
69   Chapter 4:
     Rideau Boats: A Personal View   *by James Potter*
77   Chapter 5:
     The Manotick Classic Boat Club   *by Mary Herwig and Frank Phelan*
89   Appendices:
     Photographs
     A Register of MCBC Classic and Antique Boats

ACKNOWLEDGEMENTS

This book had its genesis in 1985 in the heritage committee of the Manotick Classic Boat Club. Consisting at various times of Marlene Thomas (chairperson), Peter Elliott, Nancy Taylor, Cam Graham, Frank Phelan, Graeme Beattie, Larry Turner, Alec Douglas, Charles Marshall, Mary Herwig and Don Thomas, the committee spent many evenings pouring over old photographs, searching records and archives, designing and distributing questionnaires, cajoling members to fill them out, interviewing people, and exploring ways and means of publishing the results of this work. Marlene Thomas in particular has put an enormous amount of effort into the project and deserves our heartfelt thanks.

In the summer of 1985, thanks to a federal government grant, the club was able to employ two summer students to carry out an interview program with residents of Long Reach. Peter Davison and Bruce Bradshaw, who were in their final year of history and geography respectively at Carleton University, worked with Peter Elliott and Alec Douglas, and they gathered much useful information. In subsequent years the Ontario Heritage Foundation provided funds to pay for transcribing the interviews, thus providing a permanent record of that part of our project. We are most grateful to both the federal government and the Ontario Heritage Foundation.

Don and Marlene Thomas have been generous hosts for all committee meetings. Don also helped immensely in the provision of photographic and other supplies essential to the success of our efforts. Frank Phelan has personally vetted and copied a large proportion of the pictures in this book. His technical knowledge has been invaluable, and he has spent hours in the darkroom on our behalf. Phil and Fran Turner sorted the appendix and the Friends of the Rideau provided the map.

INTRODUCTION

The Manotick Classic Boat Club has been celebrating the heritage of recreational boating for more than a decade. A century ago people were exploring new and exciting ways to enjoy water-based recreational activity by oar, paddle, sail and steam. Looking for likely lakes and rivers, early boaters discovered the special pleasures of the historic Rideau Canal and began to lay claim to a waterway originally designed for military defence and then used for commerce and trade. This book is about the lasting links between recreational users, a wide range of boats, and the Rideau waterway.

At least since Confederation, boating activities have been celebrated in special events like regattas and in the formation of clubs and associations. Mid-Victorian athleticism was behind the creation of the Ottawa Rowing Club on an old scow at the base of the Ottawa Locks in 1867. The Perth Regatta Association initiated a long line of annual events to serve an ever-growing summer community at Rideau Ferry in 1897. In 1903, at the height of competitive rowing, sculling and canoeing, the Rideau Canoe Club opened its opulent clubhouse. With the exploding interest in gasoline-powered boats, the pioneering Ottawa Motor Boat Association was founded in 1909, with a separate branch in Smiths Falls. Concerned about lakes, islands, cottages and boats, the Big Rideau Lake Protective and Aquatic Association emerged in 1916 as a public interest group pulling together a wide range of recreational users. The Manotick Classic Boat Club inherited similar principles and interests, but the specific goal of its members was to preserve and strengthen the wooden boat heritage that lay at the foundation of recreational boating.

In the first chapter of this book Keith Dewar traces the story of recreation on the Rideau from its beginnings. Chapter 2 deals with the Long Reach section of the canal, between Burritt's Rapids and the Long Island Locks. Alec Douglas writes about people, places and events related to boating, and to the revival of antique and classic boats, on the Long Reach. In Chapter 3 Larry Turner identifies patterns of recreational boats and boaters on the waterway, with special attention to the early part of this century. Millar-Potter Restorations Ltd. of Manotick created an important focus for the revival of antique and classic boats on the Rideau, and James Potter, one of the partners, reflects on the Rideau boating tradition in Chapter 4. In Chapter 5 Frank Phelan and Mary Herwig assess the significant role of the Manotick Classic Boat Club in setting up a firm foundation of interested parties on which to build a lasting legacy of wooden boats. Finally, in an appendix, members of the Manotick Classic Boat Club contribute information on their own boats, which form part of a living museum, one that anyone can see during the navigation season, and especially on a Sunday afternoon.

Larry Turner
Commonwealth Historic
Resource Management Limited
30 January 1989

A *canoe trip in turn-of-the-century Rideau "wilderness."* – Canadian Parks Service

KEITH DEWAR
SUMMER'S TIME

The quiet drone of mosquitoes was audible in the lulls between the crashing of brush and the curse of the chain man as he moved heavily in the heat of mid-afternoon. The chief surveyor called out a stop while the Indian guide blazed the line. The surveyor wondered how anyone was going to be able to live or work in this awful wilderness. If it wasn't the swamps or thickets, it was the insects. Winter wasn't any better: cold, snow, ice. He remembered the face of his fellow surveyor who, just the winter before, had gone through the ice and drowned. "Well," he thought, as he got slowly to his feet, "at least I will be out of it and back to England at the end of the season." Measuring up fields or drawing up a line for one of the many new canals in England was a far easier way of making a living than struggling through this northern jungle.

In the beginning there were many who felt very much as our surveyor. Not only was the land a far cry from the green English countryside, with its civilized fields and manicured forests, but it was "inhabited by bears and savages." The small oases of civilization that did occur in the wilderness were often very cold comfort. Once, when Colonel John By and his staff were inspecting the works of the half-completed Rideau Canal, they spent a night in a wayside establishment where they were forced to share the meagre upstairs room with the frozen corpse of a young man who was waiting for the spring thaw to receive his proper interment. On another occasion, in the winter of 1830, a group of young gentlemen took a cutter along the frozen shore of the canal system to see how things were coming with the construction. Their lodgings were barely any better:

> The host was almost unable to speak from the effect of intoxication . . . A retreat to another inn produced this comment . . . around a table overlain with the accumulated slops and grease of many a foul but fat feast sat a parcel of lazy uncouth haggard beings the picture of indolence and sloth . . . .

The inns were bad enough, but simple travel was even worse. Winter was the only season when trips could be made with speed and some level of comfort. In the spring, knee-deep mud, insects and invisible roads made travel impossible. Summer brought heat and swamp fever, and maybe cholera. Autumn was better, but risky. Paths were often so overgrown that the chance of losing one's way was more than a little likely.

Travellers had to plan ahead with care. Usually it was best to ask at nearby settlements or in Montreal if there were any "gentlemen" pioneering in the bush through which you were to pass. Once their presence was established, it was to such little specks of civilization that you aimed, and the trip became a quick dash from one outpost to another. On the Rideau route there was Daniel Burritt at the rapids, mill owner Merrick a little further upstream, Mr. Oliver at the Perth ferry crossing, or the temperate Dr. Schofield at Portland. In those days almost every door was open; it was bad manners to refuse at the very least the hayloft — after a promise of no smoking.

The canal added a new element to travel. When that new engineering wonder came to completion in 1832, it made the trip through the roughest parts of the area much faster, allowed people to go to Montreal along the St. Lawrence – Ottawa River route, or New York City by way of the Erie Canal. And this could be done all year round. You could still stay at one of the inns, or the ever-increasing number of private homes, but the steamboat too was coming of age and offered alternate accommodation. True, the steamer of those early days was a rustic craft. In 1856 one English passenger aboard the *Prince Albert* recalled:

> She had an upper deck. Under it was the ladies' cabin, very narrow berths and a passage around it, and a gallery at the other end. Beneath it again was the gentlemen's cabin, with a row of sleeping places and a narrow dining table down the centre. The accommodation was thus very confined and rather less airy than we could have wished . . . .

All in all early travellers thought the Rideau a place of neither attractive landscape nor comfortable accommodation.

It was E.J. Baker, editor of Kingston's *British Whig*, who in 1834 gave the first hint that there might be a future recreational potential in the area. He was impressed by the canal works, suggesting that with time and a lot of work a few good mill sites could be developed. Then he added, in a back-handed compliment to the Rideau Lakes, "The sportsman might however find pleasure where no one else would look for it, for fish and fowl abound." That was the harbinger of things to come.

The recreational history of the Rideau really begins with the hunter and fisherman. The early sportsmen came for the fish and waterfowl because they were bored. Many of them were from the military bases at either end of the canal. Army life when there was no war to fight was tedious, and sport on the Rideau offered particular relief from the tedium. The canal was a military waterway manned by old soldiers who knew their duty to an officer, so what was more natural than to load up stores and a tent at Kingston or Bytown and hire a local Indian or a ruffian to take you out for a little sport? Sporadic records of these sojourns appear in the lockmasters' journals as early as 1838.

The **Rideau King** at Chaffeys Locks between 1901 and 1915. Originally built as the **James Swift** in 1893, a fire in 1901 saw the vessel transformed into a sister ship for the **Rideau Queen**. – Larry Turner Collection

The **Rideau Queen** at Jones Falls. Built by Davis Bros. at Kingston in 1900, this steamer would serve as the flagship of the Rideau Lakes Navigation Company. - Canadian Parks Service

An overkill of pike and bass. The Rideau Waterway became particularly famous for bass fishing in the drowned lands and lake trout fishing on the Big Rideau.
– Canadian Parks Service

The skiff was a fine fishing boat. Photo taken of James Evel near Smiths Falls, 24 May 1912.
– Canadian Parks Service

It was not long — although we do not know exactly how long — before a group of officers built a hunting camp several miles north of Rideau Ferry. The ruins of the buildings were still visible to passing steamboats as late as 1900. They may have been the first buildings on the Rideau put up purely for recreational purposes.

MONEY AND TIME

Interest did not go very far beyond this for about 30 years. Then, out of the ashes of the United States Civil War, arose the idea of the Rideau as a tourist haven. The expansion of northern industrial might during that conflict left a legacy of steel, steam and urban development. People moved by the thousands to the cities, with their good wages, their six-day and even five-and-a-half-day weeks. The industrial revolution had come to America.

Along with filth and squalor, and the slums that the industrial revolution brought, came the nouveau riche. The urban middle class grew as fast as the cities. It was a middle class with money and time and no income taxes, a middle class that wanted very much to emulate the old monied people of the plantations, of the grand houses of Cape Cod, and even of far-away royalty. Besides, they wanted to escape the stress and tension of business, the pressure and complexity of city life. There was a need to get back to open land and fresh air, and if Cape Cod was beyond their means they must look elsewhere, somewhere less pretentious perhaps, but nonetheless a place where one could truly recover from the trials of the workaday world.

Where could people of this class go? The Adirondacks were taken, Cape Cod was not only expensive but had class barriers (even President Grant was not welcome there). To the north, though, were Mr. Pullman's Thousand Islands, and just across the border, in that strange new Dominion, was the Rideau Canal. It was available and accesible. You could actually get there from New York City or Boston in less than 24 hours.

The American fishing gentlemen began to show up on the canal — much to the disgust of some of the lockmasters who occasionally reported groups of Americans passing their stations — in the late 1860s and early 1870s. In private conversation the term "Yankee" was used with less than endearing tones. Yet, as these strangers became more familiar figures, much of the suspicion and many of the old fears vanished. Naturally, though, no American boat was allowed on the canal without proper display of the British Union Jack. It is said that some lockmasters made a good deal of ale money selling these sporting gents the appropriate flag.

British gentlemen still came, some of them military and some just touring. Most of them still came for the hunting and fishing, but the "excursion" was becoming an accepted form of recreation too. As early as the 1830s families had taken their holidays by dashing between points of civilization, experiencing, if ever so briefly, some of the wild backwoods of Canada.

Tourists on the dock at Chaffey's Lock, 1908.
– Neil Patterson Collection, Canadian Park Service

On a Sunday afternoon, or the 4th of July. – Canadian Parks Service

The Kenney Hotel, a landmark at Jones Falls. - Keith Dewar Collection

By the 1870s many more were coming, the dash had slowed to a pleasant cruise, and the wild scenery had begun to look less frightening, even inviting. And the problem of a place to stay was no longer so difficult.

THE HOTELIERS

One of the first to recognize the possibilities offered by these growing numbers of travellers was Thomas Bartlett Kenney, who had arrived with his parents from Wexford County, Ireland, in 1855. They established a store and post office at the small community that had been built around one of the lock stations on the canal. A small operation serving the post road and the scattered settlers, it also did a little business with the small steamers that puffed their way up and down the canal. In 1877 the business was moved the hundred or so metres from the post road to the water's edge and the Kenneys began in earnest to serve the travelling public. One hundred and twelve years later, it is still owned and operated by the same family. Although it has changed, it still has the feeling expressed in this pretentious 1901 description:

> We are glad to hear again the torrent of Jones Falls and the vineclad balconies of the De Kenney House, watch its snowy waters tumble over high boulders into the lake below. This house is so largely patronised by American sportsmen that the astute host flies the Stars and Stripes and the Union Jack side by side . . . men of semi-nautical appearance lounge around and exchange fish stories after the time-honoured manner of imaginative anglers.

The De Kenney House was the same old hotel and the tumbling "snowy waters" were the overflow from the canal waste weir, but the point was made.

The Kenneys were the first, but they were soon followed by other entrepreneurs. Two lock stations down, at Chaffey's Lock, Brigett Simmons had a similar idea. The story goes that in the summer of 1886 Mr. Peter Haydon of New York asked Mrs. Simmons for room and board, for he had heard of the great fishing. He was attracted, they say, by the smell of freshly baked bread cooling on Mrs. Simmons' window sill. That was the start of the tourism industry at Chaffey's.

The industry thrives to this day. Another small hotel, owned by lockmaster William Fleming, served as a boarding house for travellers and mill workers under the management of Mrs. Lennox. In 1901 Mr. William Lashley bought the business, and it came to be known as the Idylwilde Hotel. But not everyone was happy staying at a public hotel. Some wanted a more private resort where they had control. One such group of sportsmen was from Youngstown, Ohio. They had been coming up to the Rideau for a number of years when, in 1906, they bought the Idylwilde and changed its name to the Opinicon. They purchased the building under the name of the Youngstown Hunt and Game Club, which says something about the major reason for coming to the area in the Edwardian era. The hotel remained in the hands of various club members until Donald P. Jarrett took over as the owner. He managed the hotel until his death in 1965. The resort then passed to his daughter and her husband, Mr. and Mrs. Al Cross, who still operate the enterprise in 1989.

By the turn of the century, summer resort hotels were flourishing all along the Rideau. In towns such as Westport, Portland, Newboro and Rideau Ferry, old wayside inns and taverns were converted to look after the summer visitors and fall hunters. The oldest of these wayside inns was to be found at Rideau Ferry, where it had served travellers since 1818. With the coming of the tourist trade in the 1870s, a pavilion, restaurant and lodge were added. Like all of these establishments, it had a genteel but rustic flavour. On the lawn, croquet, badminton and shuffleboard were common. For the more athletic, swimming and lawn tennis were an enjoyable way to pass a warm afternoon. On rainy days, gin rummy, cribbage, skittles, a sing-song around the slightly out-of-tune piano, lantern slides, or a book from the hotel's private library were all possibilities. Or you could just sit around the fireplace keeping the chill off and conversing with new-found friends and old acquaintances. Fishing and the next sumptuous meal were usual topics.

If the grounds got boring there were always the skiffs. These fast, stable boats were ideal for rowing one's lady fair into one of the many secluded bays. Taking a picnic basket turned the trip into something very special. The kitchen would pack cold chicken, potato salad made nippy by a bit of mustard, ham, coleslaw, fresh tomatoes, fine old cheddar from one of the many local cheese factories, fresh apple or strawberry pie, lemonade cooled with ice from the icehouse and possibly wine or stronger spirits, depending on one's personal philosophy. The ubiquitous fishing rod was often used to add fresh fish to the banquet.

You could also go on a longer excursion and have an obliging guide prepare a famous shore dinner. Most often a treat for anglers, anyone could enjoy this feast, which became legendary on the Rideau. After a morning of fresh air, to land on some tranquil spot and relax, savouring the smell of wood smoke and sizzling bass, made even the most sparing eater ravenous. Fresh fish, Canadian bacon, fried potatoes, corn on the cob, tea, carrots, radishes, cucumbers, strawberries or blueberries in fresh cream, crusty white bread and local butter were provided in abundance. The late Mrs. Jarrett of the Opinicon remarked that even if a person had a bad stomach the symptoms seemed to disappear, and such a person could consume three or even four pieces of fish without the slightest ill effect.

Whether because of the meals, the company, the fish or simply the quiet landscape, many resorts have flourished for over 90 years, and they are still going strong.

The gracious Opinicon Lodge at Chaffeys Locks in 1908. – Keith Dewar Collection

Captain Ned Fleming flanked by ladies probably on an excursion, on board the **Rideau Queen**.
– F.W. Flemming Collection, Canadian Parks Service

Dining at Hustlenit cottage near Westport on Upper Rideau Lake.
– N.B. Ballantyne Collection, Canadian Parks Service

Rowers of a skiff and paddlers of a war canoe at Hartwell's Locks, ca. 1910.
– National Archives of Canada

A PLACE OF OUR OWN

The old Victorian and Edwardian resorts were only the beginning. The beauty of the Rideau held many in its thrall, and they came back to stay for more than the few weeks at a hotel. But, for some, even the quite bustle of the hotel was too much. They still felt they were in someone else's house. For these people there was nothing for it but to buy a bit of peace and quiet and build their own palace, no matter how humble. From far away and from the local towns, people began to build their own places, usually just a camp — a piece of land with a tent and stove to start — then, at last, a real cabin. The expression "going to camp" is still used by many veterans of the Rideau system.

The Burton family typifies those who came from distant parts to stay at a resort and ended up with their own camp. The family started coming to Simmons at Chaffey's in the late 1890s. Year after year they came back, from their own home in Detroit by train to Kingston and then, by transferring to the *Rideau King* or *Rideau Queen*, on to Chaffey's. After 1918 they had the luxury of the train all the way.

Plenty of the camp owners were also from nearby towns like Perth, Smiths Falls, Kingston and Ottawa. The Hicks of Perth were one of these families under the spell of the waterway. Thomas Hicks was the proprietor of a succesful carriage factory at Perth. Before the turn of the century he had purchased a small cottage, "Sunnybank," near Beveridge's Lock on the new Tay Canal exit. His children enjoyed the soft summers and the freedom of cottage life. By the time of Thomas' death, in 1905, the cottage had begun to see better days, and the younger members of the family were growing up and leaving home. William took over the carriage works, Thomas Jr. went off to university and became a successful electrical engineer, and the three daughters took up lives of their own. But, no matter where they went or what careers they pursued, the Rideau constantly beckoned. In 1919 Thomas found what he had been looking for, a wild and beautiful point of land jutting out into Rideau Lake. He quickly purchased the property and named it Pethern Point, after the family's ancestral home in England.

The cottage, unique and built of western red cedar logs, became one of the most beautiful on the waterway. Its architecture was influenced both by the great camps on the Adirondacks and the rustic charm of Finnish log houses. The five unmarried Hicks moved in year-round, so enchanted were they with the place. As the present family historian, Larry Turner, points out, "[The] Rideau homestead was not just a place of leisure but a locale for vigorous yet refined and genteel domestic life . . . ." Servants helped with the chores in the early days, gardening, laundering, landscaping, cleaning and the like. Other buildings were added — a workshop, a root cellar, a boathouse — and a quiet shady walking trail.

Pethern Point Cottage built in 1919 by the Hicks family of Perth on Big Rideau Lake.

– Larry Turner

There was a symbiotic relationship between cottages and recreational boating. Kozy Nook cottages on the Rideau system. – Canadian Parks Service

Another unique cottage, one of the earliest on the system and known as the "Wedding Cake," was built in 1880 on Big Rideau Lake by Henry Gould of Smiths Falls. Others — "Camp Mikado," "Pine Hill," "Tree Tops," "Tigh-na-Craig," "Invernegie" — soon followed and can still be seen today.

Cottage communities sprang up all along the Rideau Canal. By the 1880s small clusters had formed at Chaffey's Lock, Rideau Ferry, Beveridge's Lock, Jones Falls, Kingston Mills, Black Rapids, Nicholson's Lock, Upper Brewers, and other spots along the route. Today a slow cottage-spotting trip along the shore of the canal can introduce the traveller to an incredibly wide variety of architecture, from the very lavish to the very humble. Each suggests something of the character of the people who built and have enjoyed them for many seasons.

The Big Rideau cottagers felt strongly enough about their beauty spot that they organized one of the first cottage associations in the province. The Rideau Lakes Protective and Aquatic Association came into being in 1916 with the objective of marking shoals, stocking the lake with fry, and generally having a voice in things. The Big Rideau Lake Association, as it is now called, still has a voice. It made itself heard in 1985, in the attempt to keep a new houseboat rental company off their lake. Many feared houseboats would spoil the beauty and tranquility of their surroundings. It is certain that the association's voice will remain strong so long as there is a lake to protect.

Wherever a camp or cottage was to be found, and however fancy, it remained a place of retreat. For the local cottage owners, when school ended in the spring the family was packed off to camp. Often the first trip of the season was made on the old *Vic 1* or the *Rideau Queen*. The boat would stop at your dock, or if the water was too shallow it would lie offshore while someone came out in the skiff to unload. Dad stayed in town during the week and rowed down from Smiths Falls Detached Lock on Saturday evening, or from Perth along the Tay Canal. Often the last part of the trip was made in the dark. Families along the shore put out lanterns for their menfolk. As the weary workers landed, lamps flickered out one by one, and the night was left to the loon, the frogs, and the chirping of crickets. The noisy new inboards, and by 1907, the even noisier outboards, put an end to this solitude forever.

For camp owners who lived farther away, the family often had to do without father for extended periods. Usually, however, everyone was in camp for the month of August.

There was a constant round of activity. Visitors came and went; picnics and parties were organized; children fished, swam and played on the water and in the surrounding forests and fields. An ice-cream run to Rideau Ferry store or Portland, only half an hour away, could take most of the day. Saturday-night dances at the local hotel were lively events that many recall with fondness — although there are those, usually the more temperate, who look back with less enthusiasm.

It wasn't all fun, but then nothing was really all work either. The lawn chairs had to be painted, the skiffs and sailboats mended and varnished, the grass, if you had any, needed occasional trimming, and the dock always wanted a little fixing. And of course there were those coal-oil-lamp chimneys that constantly demanded attention. The wasps nesting under the veranda, the squirrels in the chimney, and junior's pet frog loose in the house were all taken in stride.

These impressions reflect the general male notion of the camp, but as with all things idyllic, there was a small shadow on this happy scene. The Smiths Falls *Record News* put it best:

> One wonders whether women really liked camp life, and whether all their professed enthusiasm for it is not so much camouflage. In the case of the large majority of the occupants of these cottages and tents, they have far from comfortable quarters . . . It may be a bold assertion to make, but it is here made in all sincerity that the number of women going camping would be very small were it not fashionable to do so . . . . To married women and older daughters, who live in constant dread of snakes and poison ivy and other evils real and imaginary of outdoor life, camping is martyrdom.

It is hard to gauge the truth of such a statement, but women did not have an easy time. For the man, on his arrival at camp there was a complete change of scene. He may have had to work, but it was different at the lake, in the fresh air and open spaces. Children had summer friends, secret places, and no school. The woman was still confined by walls, kitchens, cleaning and waiting; waiting for the men to come back from fishing, waiting for children totally oblivious of time, the difference between noon and three o'clock being the blink of an eye. Unless a maid was included in the baggage, it was not so different from the trials and tribulations of home, except that there were none of the conveniences of home.

When fall finally came, everything was carefully packed, even if it were to be left for the winter, because security was important. The children packed begrudgingly, knowing that school awaited them. But the cottage's permanent residents waited for the visitors to depart. The mice would again be masters of their own domain. Food, clothes, books, anything not well protected in glass, tin or heavy wood was fair game. Goods were moved to the dock, and for the last time that summer the white flag was raised. The steamer obeyed the signal and stopped for the people and their goods. Except for an occasional weekend fishing or hunting trip, the cottage remained silent until spring.

"Stuffing Box Bill" in the sleek **ICO** *in a lock at Smiths Falls.* - Canadian Parks Service

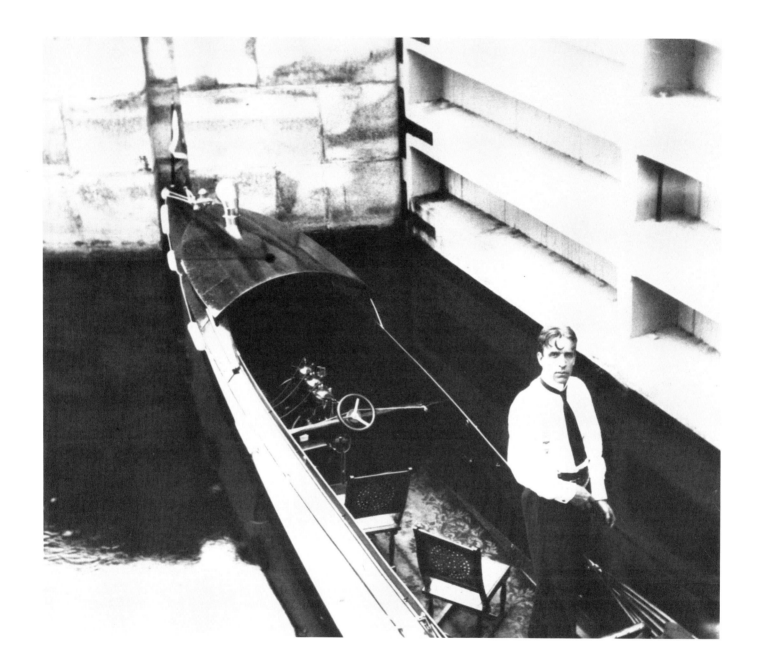

Watson's Mill at Manotick with the Canadian Ensign in the foreground. Built by Moss Kent Dickinson and Joseph Merrill Currier in 1860 this landmark is a centre of Dickinson Day festivities held on the first weekend of June every year by the Rideau Valley Conservation Authority. – Frank Phelan

ALEC DOUGLAS
THE LONG REACH

The heads of the rivers Radeau and Petite Nation communicate by short portages, or carrying places, with the waters which fall into the St. Lawrence, and promise to afford great advantages to all kinds of inland navigation . . . (Lieutenant-Governor Francis Gore of Upper Canada, 1813)

Stretch suffering from serious erosion, wake from fast boats & grazing cattle. Clays deposited in the Champlain Sea particularly prone to massive slumping after heavy rain if they have developed steep slopes. (Description of the Long Reach in *Ecotour of the Rideau Canal*, Environment Canada, 1978)

When surveyors ventured up the Rideau River from the Ottawa, towards the end of the eighteenth century, the first sizable stretch of navigable water they found was the Long Reach. About 26 miles long, it lies between Long Island, just below Manotick, and Burritt's Rapids. Since the 1960s it has been a centre of antique and classic boats.

On December 8, 1793, Edmund Burritt was born at the place that came to be called Burritt's Rapids. He was, it is said, the first non-Indian child born in the region. His father, Stephen Burritt, who had drifted down the river by raft that year, chose to settle at the rapids. At the lower end of the Long Reach, half a century later, M.K. Dickinson (the "King of the Rideau") built a mill at Long Island, and in 1859 the town of Manotick came into being. In 1829 James Lindsay settled between these two points and established a landing wharf. Burritt's Rapids, Beckett's Landing, Lindsay's Wharf, Kelly's Landing and Long Island became the stopping points for commercial vessels plying the river in the nineteenth century.

In his excellent book, *Rideau Waterway*, Robert Legget explains that the Long Reach is flanked by farmlands and that farming has gradually displaced lumbering over the years, but the farming population is decreasing. Legget says the "vigilant passenger" should watch the river banks for the main stages of farmhouse development in old Ontario. Since that advice was written. the private residences of Ottawans have encroached onto the shoreline in increasing numbers, but no matter how radical or rapid such changes may be, people and their memories stay the same. The Long Reach remains a river community and it attracts serious boaters.

Probably because it flows past gentle slopes and dairy farms rather than more spectacular scenery, this stretch of the Rideau is not so popular with tourists as more southerly parts of the river. Although there are a number of boats registered elsewhere, and some members come from other localities, most people who belong to the Manotick Classic Boat Club (MCBC) live near the village. They have made their impact on boating, and in the process the river has worked its influence on them, just as it has on everyone who has lived, worked or simply boated on the Long Reach.

Mrs. Jean Acton, for example, who runs the general store at Osgoode and was born at Kars not many years after the turn of the century, has lived a life constantly affected by the Long Reach. She was married to Doug Wallace, part owner of the Lighthouse, a popular dance hall and perhaps the most recognizable landmark along this stretch of the river from 1935 until it closed in 1967. Doug Wallace started what is now Paul's Boat Lines, which provided tours for visitors along that portion of the Rideau Canal that is within the City of Ottawa. In the 1940s Doug also established the old Rideau Ferry Inn, south of Smiths Falls on the Big Rideau. When he died, in 1949, Jean had to sell the boat tours business to Paul Duhamel, but with remarkable courage and energy she kept up the Inn until 1954.

Saturdays at the Lighthouse in its heyday were memorable. "We used to have the regattas," Jean remembers. "What a headache." Thousands of people came to race boats by day (which was one of the sources of interest in classic boats) and to dance by night. Some local clergy disapproved, but to little avail. "We had such a crowd we were afraid of the floor the first night. There was a terrible mob." Alf Boyd, born in Osgoode in 1911 and son of Doug Wallace's partner, took over management of the Lighthouse in 1945. He recalls as many as 400 people paying admission for a dance in the hall that was only 60 feet square. For five consecutive years he featured the Cliff Wilkes orchestra. (Cliff was a barber from Vernon.)

Alf Boyd had considerable enthusiasm for recreational boating. A major feature of Lighthouse activities was the annual Dominion Day regatta. In the years after the Second World War these developed into speedboat races, featuring hydroplanes and runabouts. Most of the runabouts, like Alf's own boat, a 1924 Dodge Watercar which he used for carrying passengers, were from the region. The hydroplanes came from all over the province. Noisy and colourful, these events were in a way the centre of activity for the region, until overtaken by new enthusiasms, but the link between the river and the people who used it had many other, and in some ways more enduring, forms of expression.

Along the Rideau near Kars is James Island, named after the family that farmed there and later moved to the mainland opposite. "Every year," remembers Mrs. Acton, "they used to swim their cattle over to this island in the summer. Just to let them eat the grass on the island . . . . It was terrifying to see. You know cows swim deep in the water . . . they look as if they are struggling all the time . . . ." Like many local people, Jean's own boat experience had little to do with recreation. She remembers her grandfather going out in a skiff. "He sat in the back end of it and paddled. He found that easier

The Lighthouse, built in 1915 by Doug Wallace and Harry Boyd of Osgoode. Used as a dance pavilion until 1964. Photo taken about 1950. - Alf Boyd

than rowing . . . and he would troll, and he'd be gone out every day of his life I think. He nearly always came back with a fish."

Sydney Lindsay of Kars, a direct descendant of James Lindsay, and son of the last wharfinger, Ephraim Lindsay, grew up within a stone's throw of the wharf. He and his sister, Mrs. Mrs. Bessie Edgar, have recorded their memories of the commercial traffic that took passengers and cheeses from the Lindsay wharf. Often there would be as many as 60 passengers arriving or leaving. Ephraim, who was by turns timber farmer, barn builder and carpenter, built doors, wooden tanks for cheese factories, sleighs, wagons and boats. The boats were for the most part 12-foot punts made of cedar or pine, and 10 to 14 went out of Lindsay's shop in Osgoode each year.

In 1914 or so Ephraim built what is claimed to have been the first metal-hulled pleasure boat on the Rideau. The 24-foot-long *Kars* was made of heavy-gauge galvanized iron sheets riveted to a wooden pine frame. Powered by a one-cylinder engine, it chugged along happily at the remarkably brisk rate of about 10 kilometres an hour. The family would sail to Kemptville of a Sunday to visit relatives in this splendid vessel. At about the same time, apparently, Ephraim also bought a small steamboat in a state of disrepair, installed a gas engine, and used it for two or three years himself.

The *Kars* was an oddity. Ephraim's children were much more aware of the work boats, tugs and dredges, than of boats built for leisure. The tugs *Loretta* and *Agnes* P, which continued to work until the end of the 1950s, were familiar and comfortable friends on the river. Cy Osborne, who emigrated to Canada in 1912 at the age of 18, when *Agnes* P was brand new, served as a deckhand on one of the old workboats, the dredge *Rideau*, before the First World War. The remains of the dredger, which usually plied between Ottawa and Long Island, can be seen lying on the western shore of the Rideau just downstream from Kars. When Sydney Lindsay returned to the area after the Second World War (he had been a shipwright in the navy) it was as the foreman-supervisor of maintenance and construction for the Rideau Canal. He had three Department of Transport cruisers at his disposal, but for one reason or another, perhaps because work boats were such oddities, he found them too slow for his taste.

Another old family of the Long Reach is the Kelly family of Kelly's Landing, on the east bank of the river three kilometres south of Manotick. Seven generations lie buried in the cemetery beside the Kelly home, all descended from a stonecutter who came over from Ireland to work on the Rideau Canal. Dominic Kelly, when he was interviewed in 1985, was living in the house he built in 1932, after returning from ten years teaching industrial arts in Toronto and northern Ontario. He came back to take up dairy farming and raise his ten children.

There used to be a hotel near Kelly's Landing, called by Dominic's father "the halfway house" (halfway between Manotick and Osgoode). It burned down before 1906. There was still a lot of activity there, even though the river is somewhat

Kars, built by Ephraim Lindsay. Taken from Lindsay's Wharf, 1914. Left to right: Sidney, Eph & Mildred Bessie, Marjorie & Alma. – Lindsay Family History

The flagship of Rideau Canal work boats was the **Loretta** built by Polson Iron Works of Toronto in 1907. This photo, taken in the 1920s, included Captain Ned Fleming (top) who ran the boat between 1921 and 1938. The crew were: marine engineer Ovila Seguin, who was on board from 1917 to the 1950s; Percy Leader, who died on the boat from over-exertion; John Dunn, who served 21 years as a deckhand and cook; and, fireman Steve Hayden, who worked for the Canal from 1902 to the 1940s.

– Coral Lindsay

The dipper dredge **Rideau** was acquired by the Canal in 1890. Photographed on 12 July 1914, it was a day off and the woman standing next to the washing was probably Sarah Yelland, a cook on the dredge for several years and wife of Captain James Yelland who served as Master-engineer on Rideau dredges for 49 years. This dredge was abandoned on Lake Opinicon in 1918 where it became a boarding house.

– Marine Museum of the Great Lakes at Kingston

treacherous at this point because there are deep holes through which spring water is said to bubble, and in the winter the ice is not safe. A particularly vivid memory for Dominic Kelly is of the nocturnal fish-spearing "harvests" of his youth. In early spring, after the ice was gone and before the weeds came up, people would fish the teeming shorelines with pronged metal spears for muskie, pike and sucker. They worked from boats each fitted with a metal post that supported a basket-like rack made out of metal rods by the local blacksmith. Pine roots placed in the basket and set alight illuminated the scene, and at the end of the exercise farmers and friends from miles around went home with their bran sacks full of salted fish.

Spear-fishing became illegal in the forties, but Dominic Kelly still found it worth his while to build boats. He bought 16-inch-wide cedar planks (sometimes pine) from North Gower. He would fashion the nose of a boat from a block four inches square, cut two notches into it with a circular saw, and fasten the ends of two planks to the block. That was the bow, or front of the boat. From that simple start, and using a temporary centrepiece about 40 inches wide, he would use ropes to bend the planks into shape around the centrepiece (the wood was never steamed) and screw them to a stern transom. Then he flipped the boat over and nailed planks four inches wide athwart the frame he had constructed, leaving small notches to permit the swelling that would occur in water, so that the planks would not buckle. The bottom was coated with tar. He also made his own oars, 16 feet long. It took him about three days to finish the job by this method, which he learned from another industrial arts teacher, a man of German extraction, and the only help he needed was someone to pull on the ropes. Some of his boats lasted 20 years.

In 1944 Dominic began running the tour boat *Miss Jane* for Doug Wallace, usually from the Chateau Laurier in Ottawa to Dows Lake, but occasionally all the way down to Rideau Ferry. And it was in the years following the Second World War, he recalled, that the Long Reach began to change from an uncrowded waterway, mainly populated with rowing boats, a few steamers and the odd pleasure craft, to the busy route it is now, where the number and speed of powerboats has forced property owners to build retaining walls as protection against the wakes that erode the shoreline.

Harold Saunders, who was born at Kars in 1899 and grew up on the farm the family moved to opposite Sanders Island (originally named after the family), shared many of the same memories as Dominic Kelly. He too had taken part in night-time fish-spearing expeditions, although he remembered them as a fall rather than spring activity, following the clearing of weeds. And like so many of the farmers in this area, he trapped muskrat, collecting the traps in small homemade pine boats about ten inches deep, small enough to haul over ice patches in the spring. Muskrat licences in the 1920s cost about $5, and they were not good for other animals, but Harold remembered an occasion when he caught a mink out of season. When he set it free the mink had nowhere to go, so it rode in the front of the boat until it reached dry land. At one time Harold contemplated fencing off the area around James Island as a muskrat farm, but others who tried this in the Long Reach area found the food supply inadequate for such techniques.

Harold Saunders recalled that his neighbours had a cedar canoe, and he remembered a very small houseboat, 12 feet long, that used to anchor off Sanders Island, but very few other recreational boats before 1939. Clarence Mussell, a dairy farmer who grew up on the land near the Rideau River, bears this out. He would watch his father set off in the mornings in his muskrat-trapping punt, 10 feet long and 16 inches wide, with about 2 inches of freeboard when fully loaded, and wonder how he ever prevented it from tipping in the freezing water. Reynold McGahey, a fourth-generation farmer at McGahey's Bend (a distinctive feature for boaters and named after his grandfather, even though his family used the canal less than some), remembers the small wooden rowboats made by Ephraim Lindsay, square at both ends, about 12 feet long and 4 feet wide and known for some obscure reason as "buns." Scobie Wiggins, a fifth-generation dairy farmer whose property lies across from Barnes Island on the north shore of the river, between Becketts Landing and Burritt's Rapids, remembers building his own trapping boat out of pine. Like Clarence Mussell, he put runners on the bottom for dragging it across the ice. All the old-timers agree. Punts and rowing boats were (and in some cases still are) the closest thing to recreational craft for the farmers on the Long Reach.

Clarence Curry, who after returning from military service served as a lockman at Nicholson's Lock in 1943, a bridgemaster at Burritt's Rapids from 1944 to 1956, and lockmaster at Long Island Lock until 1979, is the son of a dairy farmer from near Merrickville, south of the Long Reach, and he has witnessed as much activity on the Long Reach as anybody. He had a 27½-foot cruiser, cedar strip with an oval transom, powered with twin St. Lawrence marine engines, when he was bridge master at Burritt's Rapids. He was not the first or the only one to run this kind of boat. Almost every night he would take the cruiser out to haul a "lad" — the owner of a hotel at North Gower who came home by river in the evening — off the rocks. But in those wartime days he must have been one of the very few. On Sundays he was given two hours off to go to church, so he and his wife would make up a picnic lunch, round up 10 or 12 local youngsters, and with about five gallons of gasoline saved for the occasion, take the cruiser to Nicholson's Locks, south of the Long Reach.

But this did not stop him from other kinds of boating. Whenever he had the chance he went trapping, and as an experienced carpenter he had no problem building suitable boats for the job. During the depression, like Dominic Kelly, he had built small rowing boats (his were V-bottom boats) to rent. He recalls the sale of the *Loretta* in 1958 to private owners: "She had to be

A pastoral view of the Long Reach, about 1913. In the foreground are Edward Whelan, his wife and baby, Ambrose.

– Mr. & Mrs. Des Whalen and the Kars Women's Institute Tweedsmuir History

the slowest thing in the Dominion." As lockmaster he watched just about every kind of boat, and met just about every owner, that passed through the Long Island Locks. There were few enough before the sixties that he can recall almost every one of them.

Most owners of classic boats on the Rideau system in the forties and fifties kept and operated them in the Rideau Lakes or at the Lake Ontario end of the canal. Louis Audette of Ottawa, for example, owned a 40-foot wooden boat built in Nova Scotia, the *Kabloona*, from 1956 to 1971, and kept it in Portland. He "did" the Rideau "both ways, endless times," but preferred the stretch from Jones Falls to Smiths Falls. Scenery on the Long Reach was not so attractive, and there were long pulls between wharves. Robert Legget, who writes with such affection and grace about the entire canal, leaves a similar impression. So it is not anything remarkable about this stretch of the Rideau system that brought classic boats. What brought them to the Long Reach seems to have been the efforts of a few local residents and marina owners who shared a special interest. Syd Herwig and Jim Potter deserve particular notice.

Syd, in his own words, "was pulled out of Kilmarnock Lock with a pike pole when I was five years old, with the weeds dripping off my ears. So I was well baptised on the Rideau." His grandfather owned several inboard boats, kept at Dows Lake, and Syd was familiar with others, like the 40-foot cruiser *Wasoo* II and the Chris-Craft speedboat *Let's Go*. In the late twenties and thirties the family used to take a taxi to Dows Lake from their home in Ottawa and sail down the Rideau in a 19-foot Dolphin, a fairly beamy displacement launch built of cedar-on-oak frames, an inboard boat modified to take a low-horsepower Elto outboard. Their next boat was a 16-foot Peterborough Falcon. Syd then went off to the navy, where he had a quite remarkable career as an engine-room artificer in British "Western Isles"-class trawlers. After the war he acquired a Peterborough 16-foot runabout with a Johnson OK75 outboard, and in 1959 purchased, from Alf Boyd of Lighthouse fame, the 1924 Dodge Watercar designed by George Crouch, described by some as "the only good watercar ever built," and named it the *Calypso*. In 1967 Syd acquired a marina near Kars. It was not long before like-minded owners found their way to him. One of them was Jim Potter.

Jim Potter, who tells his story elsewhere in this book, grew up in Manotick "messing about with boats." In the forties the whistles of steamboats used to echo through his school classroom. His dad, who was in the milk transportation business, owned an 18-foot mahogany speedboat, the *Riot* II, built by Ed Andress Boat Works, Rockport, on the St. Lawrence River. Mr. Potter Sr. had also owned a Gilbert boat built in Brockville and a Peterborough. To Jim's dismay, his father sold *Riot* II when Jim was 8 years old, but the passion for classic — and fast — boats had been aroused. He went on family outings to powerboat races at Rideau Ferry. "The roar of the engines — and the marine engines of course had no mufflers on them, and the V's were

Several founding members of the Manotick Classic Boat Club at Jones Falls in 1974 en route to Clayton, N.Y. From left to right at rear: Bill Wolfe, Tony Layng, Ruth Potter, Gordon Layng; in the foreground: Linda and Charles Potter, Syd Herwig, and James Potter on the dock. – FRANK PHELAN

supercharged — was a thrilling sound," says Jim. "It made the hair stand up on end."

How Jim came to be in the restoration business, and became a founding member of the Manotick Classic Boat Club, is explained in his own account. It began in 1975, at about the same time that more people from Ottawa, many of them professionals, or in business, or public servants, began to move out to Manotick and surrounding regions. They bought their property and built their houses on or near the river, just as a revival of interest in wooden and classic boats took place across North America.

The hub of the wooden boat revival in Manotick naturally developed around the back channel leading to the Manotick Mill. Founding member John Johnston affectionately named the back bay where he lived Mahogany Harbour. Other founding members of the MCBC, John and Jim Millar of the Manotick Marina, Bob Bramwell, Peter Molin, Frank Phelan, as well as Syd Herwig and Jim Potter, used to gather informally of an evening or weekend and talk about the future of old boats. It was a matter of serious import, because they saw old boats being destroyed all around them. Several informal meetings were held on the bay at the Bob Bramwell residence, and many a night on the bay itself, sitting on their old boats. Marina owners John Millar, Jim Millar and Peter Molin were instrumental in the drive to prevent further destruction of this priceless heritage.

Other marina owners have moved in, and Syd Herwig is now retired, although still exceptionally active in the MCBC. Jim and Syd represent the closest links of the club to the early days of boating in the Long Reach. Although it still bears the characteristics of a farming community, and although trapping and fishing are still the main recreational pastimes of many residents, the Long Reach has become home to the only classic boat society in eastern Ontario.

The launching of **Cyril**, *a pre-1890 Searle rowing shell, by the Manotick Ladies Antique Rowing Club at Mahogany Harbour, Manotick, June 1986.* – Frank Phelan

Two kinds of pleasure boats. The sleek and stylish wooden skiff for the private experience and the opulent **Rideau Queen** for the public excursion.

– Kingston Picture Collection, Queens University Archives

LARRY TURNER
RIDEAU BOATING: A SPECIAL TRADITION

Boats have always played a big part in the lives of Ontarians. In a province patterned with lakes, rivers and canals, settlers arrived by boat, traded by boat, travelled by boat. It was only natural that later generations took to boats for recreation. The transformation from utilitarian to leisure craft is a story that tells us a lot about social, economic and technological change.

Ontario was an ideal location for recreational boating. When the pursuit of leisure on lakes and waterways began to evolve in the latter half of the nineteenth century, urban pressures, rising affluence and increasing free time triggered a "back to the land" movement. To the new middle class, boats and lakes became synonymous with "getting away" from the frenetic pace of business and city life. Improved transportation routes and access to the lakelands helped in their invasion of the backwoods.

Emerging at places like Niagara Falls and the St. Lawrence River, the recreational movement, at first privileged and elite, swept through diverse landscapes from Quinte and Huron shores on the Great Lakes, inland to the Kawartha Lakes, Muskokas, Georgian Bay, Haliburton, and even as far north as the Temagami regions by the turn of the century. Fed by the need to escape from urban congestion, travellers with time on their hands sought camps, cottages, hotels and steamboats in which to spend their leisure. As social custom began to release people from the guilt of not pursuing acts of religious duty or reflection in leisure time, Canadian men and women devised excuses for taking to boats, and for going to places where they could use boats.

Boats were used for observing God's gift of nature. They could be fished from. They could be propelled furiously in sporting challenge or allowed to float listlessly in placid waters. They could be lived on or carried from one place to another. The use of boats was affected by shape and style, and when new modes of power were applied to newly designed hulls, powerboats became a form of recreation, for both racing and cruising, and for pure love of the boats themselves.

Recreational boating reached new levels of popularity at the turn of the century, and contemporary with a rising sense of nationalism was a perception among Canadians that they were a virile race of beings extending the British

Arthur Jones lived, worked and played on the Rideau Canal. For 58 years he was lockman and lock-master at Smiths Falls for which he received the Imperial Service Medal in 1930. In this picture Arthur is rigging his Lake Trout fishing rod on the site of his cottage "Camp Leisure" at the entrance to Adam's Lake.

– National Archives of Canada

Empire into wild places unknown. Boating and "getting back to nature" was even considered an important element in Canada's national character. When Lou Scholes returned to Toronto with an American rowing championship in 1903, a writer was moved to comment that we were an outdoor people, fond of exercise and of fresh air, and amateur sports like rowing meant "much for the purity and supremacy of our national life, for right living and high thinking."

A writer for the small-town Perth *Expositor* in 1911 commented that man's love of water and his desire to master it in Canada "against those nations in which boats are not utilized beyond the domains of commerce and warfare, compare unfavourably in point of power and progress with the more athletic countries in which swimming and boating has attained a high degree of perfection."

Whatever the boater's motivation, just getting away from the farm, town or city for a day, week or month, and using oar, paddle or motor, was an end in itself. One of the ideal locations for such activity, although relatively unknown in the wider sphere of Ontario playgrounds, was the Rideau Waterway.

The Rideau Canal linked two major Ontario cities, Kingston and Ottawa, and two watersheds, Lake Ontario and the Ottawa River. The Rideau system offered island-studded lakes, narrow man-made channels, flowing rivers and pastoral lock sites along its length. It travelled through rural landscape and isolated forests, and visited many villages and towns in its path. There was excellent water for canoeing, sailing and boat racing. The drowned lands and wetlands were famous to hunters who were after waterfowl. Fishing spots in deep, cold lakes, spring-fed waters and shallow, stump-infested bass pools made the Rideau an angler's paradise. The aging canal offered passage for travelling boaters, and at certain locations there were hotels, camps and cottages where boats could be kept.

The Rideau Waterway did have its limitations — Montreal and Toronto for example had closer playgrounds — but it was ideal for Ottawa and, to a lesser degree, Kingston. At first, it is true, boating was concentrated on the Ottawa River to the north and the St. Lawrence and Lake Ontario to the south. The Rideau Canal, although it entered into the heart of Ottawa, was separated from the city at the Kingston end by a stumpy, weedy marsh. In areas where flooding was necessary to build the canal, the channel wound its way amidst the drowned lands. Even as late as the 1950s, the Rideau had not lost its reputation as a difficult system to navigate, with the requirement of guides for craft as small as fishing skiffs and as large as steam yachts and cruisers. It was also a shallow draft canal in its cut and locks. Stories of stranded yachts in difficult passages before the improvement of channel-marking and clearing in this century did little to help public relations.

The Rideau was poorly served by railway before 1913. Nevertheless, Americans had discovered the system when the Brockville & Westport Railway was built in 1884, by its close proximity to the popular St. Lawrence, and by

The Rideau Canoe Club was formed in 1902 with only 20 members but by 1905 it had erected this magnificent clubhouse on the canal driveway in Ottawa.

– National Archives of Canada

the scheduled trips of the opulent *Rideau King* and *Rideau Queen* in connection with the New York Central Railway after 1900.

Within the system, boating, when not involving canal-length trips, centred mostly on vacation areas in the interior, like Rideau Ferry, Portland, Westport, Newboro, Chaffey's Locks and Jones Falls. The focus was on cottages, camps and hotels, and in particular on people holidaying from the nearby towns of Perth and Smiths Falls. The Rideau system also attracted people from Ottawa, but not from other major cities in Canada. Consequently the Rideau developed a boating tradition of its own, one that offered a beautiful and varying landscape, patronized by a uniquely cloistered vacation community that came from the Rideau system itself and the Ottawa Valley. A growing community of American vacationers and sportsmen were especially significant in the southern lakes, and there were important recreational communities established at the Hogs Back, Mooney's Bay, Long Reach, Burritt's Rapids and Brewers Mills sections of the canal. However it was the lake district itself which received the greatest recreational pressure, often centred around lock, bridge or village sites.

At either end of the canal, recreational boating had its beginnings in athletic competition. Military regattas in Kingston and Ottawa from the 1850s anticipated a subsequent interest by the general community. Boatbuilders in places like Barriefield and Ottawa were constructing racing sculls and their like by the 1880s.

By that time racing had largely been overtaken by general interest in canoes, skiffs and sailing craft of all shapes and sizes. Competition still thrived, as witnessed by the development of such organizations as the Ottawa Rowing Club in 1867, the Kingston Rowing Club in 1881, the Rideau Canoe Club and the Smiths Falls Canoe Club in 1902. These and other organizations encouraged all kinds of boating, especially in the celebration of summer regattas. The development of a lightweight rowing skiff easily used by fishermen, or for quiet outings in the Adirondack and St. Lawrence regions, was matched by the creation of somewhat stable wooden canoes based on Indian design in the Peterborough and Maine areas. These small craft helped initiate and make more pleasant a leisure-seeking person's discovery of the waterway. The access made possible by skiffs and canoes encouraged the rise of temporary vacation camps on the lakeshore, the precursor to cottages.

The rowing skiff was an all-purpose boat at camp, cottage or hotel. Rideau skiffs were similar to the double-ended Adirondack – St. Lawrence varieties, sleek wooden craft approximately 18 to 22 feet in length and 40 to 50 inches in the beam. The Rideau skiff tended to have lower gunwhales and wider seats to accommodate their widespread use as fishing boats. The skiff was particularly flexible in shallow bass ponds, where it could float over drowned stumps with stealth and silence. In the smaller lakes and channels in the vicinity of Newboro, Chaffey's Locks and Jones Falls, a

Unidentified couple in **Randall M.** at Chaffeys Lock, 1908.
- Neil Patterson Collection, Canadian Parks Service

Period clothing and recreational boating were not an easy match. Mrs. Morgan, sister of the wife of Smiths Falls Detached Lockmaster Arthur Jones, is settled into an Adirondack style canoe. - Canadian Parks Service

The skiff was an all purpose boat. Photograph taken on the Rideau Canal near the CNR Bridge in Ottawa East.
- N.B. Ballantyne Collection, Canadian Parks Service

This boat on the Rideau Canal in Ottawa is possibly a 1924-25 twenty-four foot Peterborough Watercraft. The identical model was also built by Gilbert Boat Works of Brockville, Ontario. – National Archives of Canada

frequent sight at daybreak was a line of skiffs being towed by a larger boat full of fishermen and their guides, intent on angling for bass.

Several Rideau boatbuilders, including Nichol of Smiths Falls, Dowsett of Portland, Conley of Westport, Lyons of Newboro, Alford of Chaffey's Locks, Patterson of Elgin, and the Dey and Knapp families of Ottawa and Kingston–Barriefield areas respectively, made important contributions to the heritage of Rideau skiff-building between 1880 and 1940. The precision and skill of wooden boat makers allowed skiffs to be designed with exotic varnished wood on gunwhales and planked with red cedar, white pine, mahogany, black cherry, black walnut or butternut. The skiff was a flexible boat that made a transition into sailing and motorboating, especially in the latter case with the development of the disappearing-propeller boat after 1916.

The canoe required a little more skill and stability to navigate than did the skiff, but its widespread popularity continues to the present day. They served as functional boats for camp and cottage, and their portability was significant for planning overnight excursions and trips. Indeed the Rideau was and still is an excellent location for canoe-tripping by families, groups and youth camps. The typical canoe used on the Rideau system would have been a 14- to 16-foot-long cedar-strip or wood-and-canvas boat built by either the Peterborough Canoe Company or the Chestnut Canoe Company of Fredericton, New Brunswick. These two companies dominated the Canadian canoe market until the 1960s, but there were other small builders involved as well. The war canoe, with as many as 16 or more paddlers on board, was a regatta favourite between competing clubs at the turn of the century. These long, distinctive canoes were even used for tripping, as in 1905, when a war canoe from St. Rose, Quebec, made a round trip using the Rideau. As a recreational boat the canoe was an effective leap to the past, carrying symbolic images of native heritage, the *coureur du bois* and the exploration of Canada's wilderness.

While the canoe and skiff offered a personal and private means of access to the waterway, most travellers would have their first taste of the Rideau on a steamboat. Steamers had plied the length of the Rideau from its opening in 1832. The early steamers hauled freight and passengers from place to place. Passengers were on board for business or personal travel, and many were immigrants en route to their new homes. The odd recreational traveller did use the steamers, perhaps a journalist writing about the hinterland or a visiting adventurer seeking new sights. Steamer service on the waterway went into decline after Confederation, but a revival took place in the 1880s with a new-found interest in the Rideau Waterway's fresh lake breezes and wonderful scenery, and as a focus for excursions.

The rage for excursions seemed to flow in from the St. Lawrence River and its vacation areas. Large steamers found new business in luxury excursions, and some old passenger ships turned into opulent craft for overnight or

Owing to long distances and lockages between some bass pools and resorts, a service was often provided by hotels to have a motor boat tow a string of skiffs, guides and fishermen to their secluded sites. A group is getting ready to depart in this historic photo. - Neil Patterson Collection, Canadian Parks Service

The **Olive** was built in Smiths Falls in 1875 by William O'Mara. Although very much a "freighter" it became a popular excursion boat in the 1890s.

– National Archives of Canada

day trips. By 1894 the Rideau was traversed by several boats sporting new interior fittings for scheduled trips and wide open spaces for excursions. Such boats included the *Rideau Belle*, *James Swift*, *Olive*, *John Haggart*, *Ida*, and some St. Lawrence boats, such as the *Brockville* and *Aletha*, which were able to squeeze into the Rideau locks. Many of these earlier boats were large, having three decks and ample space for overnight accommodation. They tended to specialize in canal-length exursions and circular trips calling at Kingston, Ottawa and Montreal.

Late Victorian and Edwardian lakeside recreation has been described by Joseph Schull as society going afloat "in moonlit steamer excursions and rowing matches and regattas, while band concerts and picnics enlivened the public parks." Author Stephen Leacock evoked a sense of the excursion experience in his charming *Sunshine Sketches of a Little Town*:

> I suppose that all excursions when they start are much the same. Anyway, on the *Mariposa Belle* everybody went running up and down all over the boat with deck chairs and camp stools and baskets, and found places to sit, and then got scared off again. People hunted for places out of the sun and when they got them they weren't going to freeze to please anybody; and the people in the sun said they hadn't paid fifty cents to be roasted. Others said they hadn't paid fifty cents to be covered with cinders, and there were still others who hadn't paid fifty cents to get shaken to death with the propeller.

An excursion trip on a steamer was very much a public spectacle. Men and boys would dress in their Sunday finest; women and girls would carry white parasols and don flowing shawls. Excursions were held for holidays, special celebrations, church picnics, business and trade outings, and any excuse for the gathering of a group of people to charter a steamer large enough to handle their crowd.

The stately cabin steamers famous for overnight and day-use excursions were the *Rideau Queen*, launched in 1900, and the *Rideau King*, which was rebuilt in 1901 from the burned-out remnants of the *James Swift*. Both were built in Kingston and operated by the Rideau Lakes Navigation Company, which focussed its marketing on American tourists. In 1904 a sixteen-year-old visiting his grandfather's cottage recalled a Masonic excursion from Perth on the *Rideau King*:

> The three decks were crowded and a lot of people had not seats. After we started from the locks we soon reached Rideau Ferry. A lot of people had tickets bought here and were all ready to get on. The boat was so crowded that only half were allowed on .... Newboro is 25 miles up the lake and as we had never been up more than 10 or 12 miles we enjoyed the trip fine as the scenery on the Upper Rideau Lake is magnificent. On the top deck the Perth Citizens Band enlivened the crowd with music and on the second deck the piano and violin chimed in together. Now and then we would meet a yacht and would salute it. Again we would catch sight of a family of loons

swimming around near the boat and when we reached Rocky Narrows the fishermen could be seen hauling in the big salmon. The three of us enjoyed the sun on the top deck where the band was and enjoyed the sun and wind . . . . After locking through the Narrows Locks we soon reached Newboro at 1:15. On the boat we bought a lot of peanuts and had a time eating them. At Newboro wharf the Brass Band of that place escorted the people up town . . . . At quarter after three the King blew and at 3:30 we were on our way home.

The importance of the day outing for people living at inland towns such as Perth and Smiths Falls encouraged the use of smaller, more practical steamboats.

The dual-purpose steamer, around 60 feet in length, was well suited for Rideau Lakes traffic. Just the right size for local town trade and servicing the recreational community, the boats could also be used for scheduled or chartered excursions. Boats such as the *Aileen* and *Antelope* had single decks and freight holds, and could squeeze almost 100 on board for an excursion but normally had no room for overnight accommodation. Freight was stored on a lower deck and people on an upper deck. Some of the smaller steamers were built on the Rideau, but William Robinson, the Davis Dry Dock Company, and other Kingston builders, were responsible for many more.

The steam yacht was a natural variation of a larger steamer, except that with the introduction of naptha gas and the replacement of bulky coal by 1883, it was possible to reduce engine size and increase safety. The private use of small steamers was complemented by a public demand for seasonal "town boats." Both in Smiths Falls, under the tutelage of George Davis, and in Perth, with the entrepreneurship of Peter Cavanagh, a line of smaller excursion boats was established. Using both dual-purpose steamers and steam yachts, Davis and Cavanagh were able to service a local Rideau Lakes market involving cottage and hotel supplies, town trade, scheduled and chartered excursions, and scheduled passenger runs. Steam yachts for public use, like the *Tropic* of Smiths Falls, or *Arrah Wanna* and *St. Louis*, and in Smiths Falls, boats like the *Iola*, *Lee*, *Antelope*, *Buena Vista*, *Stranger*, *Princess Louise* and the *Victoria*, traversed the inner sanctum of Rideau waters. Some steam yachts were built on the Rideau by William O'Mara of Smiths Falls and Hugh Harold of Rideau Ferry.

The colourful steamboat and excursion era on the Rideau Canal was short-lived. After peaking in the first decade of the century, cabin steamers were effectively eliminated by the end of the First World War. The great Northern Railway, which passed through the heart of the Rideau Lakes in 1913, provided a new form of access that made the large boats obsolete. Railways, steamers and hotels on the Rideau never developed the amount of mutual support that they did elsewhere. Even the small steamers had been largely eliminated by 1920. Cavanagh had gone out of business. Davis did maintain the *Victoria*, and the later gasoline-

The ***Iola*** was the first steam yacht operated by George Davis of Smiths Falls in a town boat service to the Rideau Lakes. Using several steam and gasoline powered boats between 1904 and 1942, Davis developed a passenger, excursion and local freight service into a consistent enterprise.

– G.R. Davis Collection, Canadian Parks Service

An elegant and luxurious steam yacht tied up at Chaffey's Locks in 1908.
– Neil Patterson Collection, Canadian Parks Service

*The steam yacht **Phoebe** was a sleek boat on the Rideau Canal.*
– Canadian Parks Service

powered *Victoria* II, until the 1940s, and the steamer *Ottawan* continued a limited service up to 1933, but the Rideau simply could not sustain public boats in the face of competition from the automobile (using improved and more numerous roads) and motorboating. These changed the transportation needs of the vacationing public.

The steam yacht was the first recreational motorboat. Its elegance, exclusiveness and technology were very much part of the nineteenth century, but it anticipated the emphasis on comfort, luxury, leisure, and the private enjoyment of nature's waterways that were part and parcel of pleasure boating in the twentieth century. Several steam yachts visited the Rideau Canal from the United States in the late 1870s, and by the 1880s several had found their way into the hands of Rideau cottagers. Seventeen steam yachts were counted at the Rideau Ferry regatta in 1901, including the *Nellie*, *Katie*, *Roy Barnes*, *Kilburn* and *Heavenly Rest*, all from Smiths Falls; the *Dorothea* from Brockville; the *Genesee* of Rochester, N.Y.; the *Weary Waggles* of Ottawa; the *Eva Belle* and *Jopl* of Westport; the *Dorothy* of Rideau Ferry; and the *Geraldine*, *Winona*, *Cygne* and *Bessie* from Perth, the *Bessie* heralding a new age of motorboats, equipped with an internal-combustion gas engine.

The steam yacht could be a simple boat, or it could be the height of luxury. The little steamer widened the horizon of Rideau boating by making canal trips possible. Lock gates no longer became blockages, but opened up new vistas for boating. Steam yachts, because they were well designed for canal travel, provided the impetus for further boating. After preparing the engine and stoking the fire, one did not just go for a spin, one went somewhere. The boats were easy to moor near camp or cottage sites, and their mobility foreshadowed both the individuality of later boating and the rise of the cruiser so prevalent on the canal today.

The public nature of the excursion experience gradually gave way to the private pursuit of pleasure boating. The canoe and skiff made this possible from one end of the spectrum, and the steam yacht from the other. In between were a number of variations.

One of the most interesting variations on steam yachts, and later of cruisers, was houseboats. There was a proliferation of them at the turn of the century as people attempted to bring the comfortable and convenient urban style with them on holidays. Houseboats were like mobile cottages. At first they depended on steam yachts for a tow, and their awkwardness in wide lakes subject to wind confined most of them to narrow channels and cuts in the southern portion of the canal. An example of one of these boats, once called the *Wenona* but now the *Ark*, rests contentedly on shore near Upper Brewers Locks. The houseboats was largely supplanted by the high-powered planing cruiser, able to take house and home on fast trips, but the idea of the mobile cottage did not wane and in recent years the Rideau has experienced a revival of the houseboat, the modern self-powered version.

Sailing craft were popular on the Rideau Lakes, but they did not establish themselves to the same extent as in the St. Lawrence, at Kingston, or on the Bay of Quinte. Confined to the centre of the system, and rarely venturing beyond lock stations, sailboats were seldom used for touring. The narrow channel and shallow river sections of the canal were not conducive to sailing, although sails were often rigged in canoes, skiffs and dinghies. These were usually makeshift arrangements. Craft designed for sailing were frequently part of a cottage fleet. In the modern era sailboat designs have brought many different classes of boats to the Rideau system, handling waters that sailors once described as treacherous.

The next revolution came with the internal-combustion engine. Faster than steam and safer than naptha, gasoline motors were the technological answer to the craving among recreational boaters for a fast, efficient and convenient vessel. Motorboats served all tastes. They could run slowly or at speed; they could be all-purpose utility boats, fishing craft, touring boats, racing boats, or dream machines offering a new horizon to their owners. Motorboats became a means of enjoying the lakeland with the least amount of effort. And they were often objects of delight in themselves.

They arrived on the Rideau Canal precisely at the turn of the century, when, in 1901, Thomas Hicks floated the *Bessie* in the Tay Canal. In 1905 the magazine *Rod and Gun in Canada* reported that "gasoline launches are now all the rage." In 1908 there were 41 motorboats in Perth and 36 in Smiths Falls. When a Mr. M.L. Lapointe purchased a new gasoline yacht that same year, the Perth *Expositor* commented that it was a real "peach": "It has the speed, is roomy, safe, and is equipped with one of the latest model engines on the market." Motorboat lockages on the Rideau Canal increased from 14,882 in 1910 to 24,884 in 1915.

The increasing number and availability of motorboats were major incentives in the revival of the Rideau Ferry regatta, which had first run in 1897. Interest fell off after 1904, but in 1909 organizers of the new regatta featured motorboat racing, and this attracted 2,000 people. There was also a night-time flotilla of illuminated boats, not an easy accomplishment with the inflammability of early gasoline mixtures.

Organizations like a boating club at Rideau Ferry, and the Ottawa Motor Boating Association, formed in 1909, encouraged the staging of regattas with the emphasis on motorboating. The Ottawa club's membership skyrocketed with the early popularity of cruising on the section of the canal from Dows Lake to Ottawa Locks. In 1915 the Ottawa club and the Smiths Falls Motor Boat Association backed a regatta at Portland, and it was partly to repeat this event the following year that the Rideau Lakes Protective and Aquatic Association was created. When the Rideau Ferry regatta was revived for a third time, it was at the behest of a newly formed Rideau Ferry Aquatic and Motor Boat Association, in 1922.

Regatta day at Rideau Ferry was centred around the old Coutts House hotel, later becoming the Rideau Ferry Inn. – Larry Turner Collection

The **Gwen** was built in Westport for Merrickville industrialist T.W. Watchorn. Its hull is designed for slower and bulkier steam power but it is gasoline driven. The fixed canopy reflects the slow speed of early gas engines.
– G.R. Davis Collection, Canadian Parks Service

Pursuit of pleasure boating knew no borders. The rounded hull of this early motorboat was typical before speed and engine size forced new streamlined hulls.
– Canadian Parks Service

The nature of regattas held at this period is indicated by the trophies awarded. At Portland in 1920, for example, these included the Beardmore Trophy for sailing, the Edwards Trophy for the single-cylinder motor skiff, the Ogden Trophy for the limited 15-inch cubic motor, the Kingsmill Trophy for the runabout handicap, the Carson Trophy for the double-cylinder motor skiff, the Freiman Trophy for the association handicap (average speed 19 m.p.h.), and the Workman Trophy for the open 12-mile event.

Motorboats could not easily be pulled up on shore, like canoes or skiffs, and an enduring legacy of their use was the erection of boathouses and the later development of marinas for maintenance and storage. Near Ottawa, the development of large, many-stalled boathouses run by private boating clubs was the first step towards the rise of the marinas. Little is left of the rows of makeshift boathouses that used to cluster near towns and villages. By 1921 an estimated 700 boathouses had been built along Rideau waters, including 210 on canal property. Boathouse regulations, speed controls, lockage priority, channel marking, fish patrols and boater safety were only a few of many points of discussion, and sometimes disagreement, between boaters, canal administrators and government agencies.

"Small, sporting, snorting, coughing, roaring, farting," as the novelist Robertson Davies described them, the first internal-combustion engines and the boats they powered enjoyed instant success, in spite of their undoubted flaws. In 1905 the Perth *Courier* described an interrupted outing on the Tay Canal:

> A small party of gentlemen were down the river in a gasoline launch, Saturday evening, and met with a disappointing occurrence. The gasoline yacht gave out and they had to use seats to paddle to Dowsens where they left the craft and footed it home.

And if the reliability of motorboats was dubious, their noise was all too indisputable. In 1911 a cottager urged neighbours to get together for a protest meeting against the "ear-breaking nerve-wracking noise that some of the motorboats make."

The protest evidently had little effect. A nice description of activities on the Rideau Canal, in the August 7, 1913, issue of the Smiths Falls *Rideau Record*, makes this clear:

> All day long and sometimes part of the night the sound of the noisy little launches is everywhere, but they are in high favour, noise and all, or perhaps it ought to be said in spite of the noise. They are the product of the last ten or fifteen years, but now seem almost indispensable. They are on the Rideau in all shapes or sizes and go careening through the water from four miles an hour to twenty. They have all kinds of original names such as "We Two", "No Hurry", "Ronomore" and are really one of the best modern inventions when they are run with the exhaust under water. Besides these, the lake is alive with row boats in

which carefree men and women pursue the fish or drift aimlessly about killing time and getting pleasure doing it.

A number of Rideau boatbuilders participated in the early development of motorboats. It is true that rapidly changing technologies in engine and hull design tended to cause boatbuilding, like automobile manufacturing, to become centralized in urban areas. Nevertheless, the continued use of wood encouraged pockets of excellence to flourish away from the largest towns and cities, in places like Barriefield, near Kingston, and in the Muskoka region of Ontario, where the Ontario boatbuilding tradition reached its peak of perfection. Thus as the rise of motorboating occurred, many kinds of boats, bearing the names of companies large and small throughout Ontario and the northeastern United States, found their way to Rideau waters.

Exciting technological changes, widely influenced by experimentation in racing, have occurred throughout this century. Wooden boat hulls, formed from rounded patterns designed to handle the weight and load of steam engines, developed into tube-like hulls built for large gasoline engines and for speed. Increased speed

*Note the sleek sheer line on the motorboat **Mitzi** as it leaves the locks at Kingston Mills in 1914.*
- R.K. Odell Collection, National Archives of Canada

The **Alice E.** reflects changes in motorboat hull design. The wide round hull is now narrow and tubular, designed to cut through water with faster engines.
– Neil Patterson, Pennock Collection, Canadian Parks Service

Motorboat racing helped develop new engines and hull design. A major contribution was the planing hull allowing boats to skim over the water rather than push through it. This Canadian speedboat was the **Tempo VII**.

and mobility resulted from the development of the V-shaped hull, and later planing hulls which skimmed over the surface. Corresponding portability, speed adjustments and gasoline mixtures influenced boat design and made it compatible with the different purposes to which boats were being put. Like automobiles early in the century, motorboats were at the cutting edge of technological change in engine propulsion and hull design.

Interior design and style was also important in boat development. The open spaces in early round-hulled motorboats soon gave way to covered decks in tube-shaped designs. Engine displacement and location affected boat interiors. When engines became more compact and powerful they were moved from fore to aft. This shortened the required length of boats and allowed the hull to be wider, for maximum planing on the water surface. The stubby, wide, close-decked runabout of the 1930s became a standard boat on Ontario waters, whether powered by an inboard or an outboard engine.

As motors became smaller, lighter and faster, the transition was made to the outboard. That put *finis* to the double-ended skiff which had absorbed the engine in its hull. The new outboard engine had such portability that it could not be resisted by boaters. The popularity of outboard motors attached to square-ended skiffs or rowing boats knew no bounds in the 1920s and 30s, and the outboard has grown since then to handle several sizes of boats with increasing power.

With the improving designs of planing boat hulls, powerful engines were attached to larger boats, creating a cruiser class with cabins and extra decks on board. The artistry in design of wooden-hulled boats slowly gave way to simpler and often lighter metal and fibreglass boats which demanded much less maintenance time for busy cottage users. Rapid technological change, mass production and the marketing methods of large-scale producers selling cheaper and easier-to-handle metallic boats led to the loss of local boatbuilding artisans and the rise of marina-based sales agencies. Although companies building wooden-hulled boats survived into the 1960s, as did some local builders, the cheaper and more efficient metal and plastic boats dominated the market.

Throughout western history people have sought leisure in boats of every different shape and size, and for many different purposes, so it is true to say that the design and use of recreational boats is an expression of culture. Olympic events, for example, are held in sailing, rowing and canoeing. The America's Cup captures world attention every three years. In Ontario, it would be impossible to talk about public use of the lakelands without an attempt to consider the role and contribution of boats to recreational development. Adapting boats for use in pleasure has strongly influenced our perception of the landscape. Public access to waterways, and how people have used boats there, has given us a new awareness of lands in their natural state as places of recreation, rather than simply foundations for industrial, agricultural or resource development.

Clockwise: The outboard motor. Its popularity and portability influenced the design of square-ended boats. – Frank Phelan

A wooden skiff next to its historical replacement, the square-ended boat with outboard motor. Photo from the 1983 Alexandria Bay Boat Show. – Frank Phelan

Add a portable outboard engine to a simple wooden boat and boating became suddenly more accessible and easier for recreationists after 1920. Ed Hendee's boat and motor were photographed at the Perth Show in 1984.
– Frank Phelan

Bert Clouthier's **Rideau Prowler** is representative of an era that combined powerful new engines with sleek hull design and luxurious accommodation to create the classic cruiser. Dows Lake 1986. – Frank Phelan

The Rideau Canal, these days, exists for boaters more than anything else. Its transformation from military by-pass to commercial route, and then to recreational waterway, reflects changing patterns of the times. Stately steamers are now extinct, and the summer waters are alive with plastic, rubber, kevlar, fibreglass, steel, aluminum and, to a decreasing extent, wooden boats.

In the craze for convenience and portability, and the search for affordable prices, many old wooden boats have been left aside to rot. They represent the formative years of recreational boating on the Rideau. Some were built in shops along the shores of the river and canal before the era of mass production. The world of wood governed tastes and designs in that era, and the sense of craftsmanship and pride in their building constitute an important part of our heritage.

The special tradition of Rideau boating, which as the previous chapter explains has found a focus on the Long Reach section of the waterway, has its roots in those formative years. It finds expression in the artistry, survival and restoration of the early wooden boats. This is an activity that adds dignity and charm to pleasure boating because it captures the durability in form, and delight in design, that went into the construction of the vessels; because it nourishes the spirit of discovery that led to their preservation; and because it provides the satisfaction of having preserved a thing that combines such profitable use with such striking beauty.

The author would like to acknowledge permission by the Canadian Parks Service to use material from his report "Recreational Boating on the Rideau Waterway, 1890-1930," Microfiche Report 253, (1986), and for time granted by his employer, Commonwealth Historic Resource Management Limited, to write this article.

JIM POTTER
BOAT BUILDING ON THE RIDEAU: A PERSONAL VIEW

My name is James Potter. I was born in Manotick just before World War II. In 1842 our family settled on the 1st Line of Kars, near the village of Manotick, and I am still on that original piece of land. My partner, John Millar, and I are in the boat restoration business. Wooden boats have come to be part of my life for many reasons, the first of which is that they form a very strong part of eastern Ontario's heritage.

It is a well-known fact among wooden boat collectors that boats manufactured in Ontario, because of its abundance of freshwater lakes, are among the finest watercraft built in the world. It is also well known that from 1910 to 1960 boatbuilding was one of Ontario's largest industries. Some of these esteemed builders were in our Golden Triangle area.

Gilbert Boats of Brockville, Ontario, operated between approximately 1910 and 1940, building skiffs and luxury launches. They also acted as the distributors of Dodge Boats of Detroit, Michigan. From 1905 to 1935 Malette Boats of Gananoque produced fine skiffs and launches, of which several are still in service. Myles Jeffrey, who worked for Chris Smith of Chris-Craft fame from 1920 to 1930, the era of *Baby Reliance* and the Gar Wood *Miss America* Gold Cup and Harmsworth Trophy and record holders, returned to Athens, Ontario, near Charleston Lake, about 1934. He built his own luxury speedboats until his retirement circa 1953. His production, working almost single-handedly, was possibly as many as 50 custom speedboats, of which probably 15 are still in use.

W. Ed and Elmer Andress had their yard at Rockport, Ontario, still operated by a grandson, Dick Johnson. Andress built many St. Lawrence skiffs, tour boats and launches. Ed Andress was about 95 when he died on December 30, 1981. Between 1900 and 1940 the Dowsett yard of Portland, on Rideau Lake, built rowing boats, motor skiffs, and beautiful mahogany launches. About 15 Dowsett launches are still in use. At Smiths Falls, between 1915 and 1935, Davy Nichols built some of the finest-crafted skiffs and launches anywhere in North America. Another Smiths Falls builder was Ernie McEwen, who produced runabouts and racing boats.

My introduction to this world of boating was through my father. He was encouraged to continue in the family tradition of farming, and a good farm was acquired for him by his father, but he found that farming was not to his liking

Two Rideau beauties. In the forefront the Moore family in **Rideau Passage**, a motor launch built by Davy Nichol at Smiths Falls in 1915. The Sneyd family are riding in the motor launch **Gran D** which was built in 1928 by Dowsett of Portland. Photo taken at the Perth Basin, 1984. – Canadian Parks Service

and as a result entered into the milk transportation business just after the Depression, as there was a service to be provided, hauling producers' milk into the Ottawa market.

My father was a gregarious and personable man. Early on in his career he became interested in speedboats, which were very popular at the time. He took every opportunity to attend boat races at Alexandria Bay, Brockville, or any other location within a day's drive which hosted these activities. As my father's enthusiasm grew for this exciting world of speedboats, he felt compelled to commission a new boat to be built for him by the Gilbert Boat Company of Brockville, in 1938 I believe. He married my mother, Pearl Simpson, the same year and in the early spring of 1939, shortly after the river was opened for navigation, my mother and father took their honeymoon in a waterfront cottage near Maitland, Ontario, where they also took delivery of their boat.

The boat was a 20-foot runabout, quite beautiful, but not all the details had been attended to and my mother, an inexperienced operator, was consequently compelled to run the boat upstream to Brockville and back for a few trips to iron out the final adjustments. Subsequently, after many trips to the Gilbert Boat Company and back to Maitland, and many explanations as to why this was necessary, the boat was named *Excuse*. The *Excuse* finally made it to her home port of Manotick, and she was beautiful, but unfortunately she was destroyed by fire at her Manotick mooring in her first full season. The cause of the fire remains a mystery.

In the course of the construction of *Excuse* my mother and father became friends with Fred Gilbert, and as he was an official at boat races at Alexandria Bay, I am told, they attended many boat races together.

In about 1940 my father purchased another boat, which I understand was a 20-foot twin-cockpit Peterborough which he named *Riot*, probably after the series of *Riot* boats involved with racing and with speedboat rides which were running for hire on the St. Lawrence River at that time. I believe it was in 1940 or 1941 that my parents met Doug and Jean Wallace of Osgoode, who owned the Lighthouse on the Rideau River at Osgoode. Doug was a speedboat fan, too, who initiated a tourboat service and speedboat rides from this location, and operated a boat livery with canoes and rowboats for rent during World War II. This bustling business was enhanced by Saturday-night dances at the famous Lighthouse pavilion.

The two mahogany tour boats Doug Wallace owned and used for weekend cruises on the Rideau, the *Miss Barbara* and *Miss Jane*, were beautifully styled and finished in light varnish. They were built by Ed Andress and Sons of Rockport, on the St. Lawrence. My father, who by this time had discovered that the performance of *Riot* was not satisfactory, as he always seemed to be riding a wake, purchased a new runabout from Ed Andress and named it *Riot* II. *Riot* II was an exceptionally fast 18-foot twin-cockpit runabout with a V-bottom, powered by a St. Lawrence Marine V-8 Ford conversion.

Apparently it is one of only two V-bottom boats that Ed Andress ever built. This is the boat that I remember as a child, the one that instilled in me forever a love of fast mahogany boats.

Another friend of my parents was the late Paul Duhamel, who after the war was employed as a driver for Colonial Coach Lines of Ottawa, now Voyageur Colonial. His interest in boats led him to purchase a site at Hogs Back, on the Rideau near Ottawa. He started a boat livery and rental business, and ultimately bought the tour boats *Jane* and *Barbara*, put them into service on the Ottawa canal, and formed the now famous Paul's Boat Lines, run today by his sons Dan and John. I must say the *Barbara* and *Jane* were much more graceful of form than the large steel high-capacity hulls they are presently using. One of the old Andress hulls is still lying in Duhamel's yard in Manotick and may someday be restored for posterity and used for private or executive tours.

My father, who really enjoyed the performance of *Riot* II, competed in impromptu racing at the Lighthouse, and in the Service Class Runabout, APBA (American Power Boat Association) racing at Rideau Ferry Inn after it was purchased by Doug Wallace. This was the scene of exciting boat races for people on the Rideau Waterway, sometimes attended by 8,000 to 10,000 spectators.

Boat races had been held at Rideau Ferry since 1897, and with some interruptions and many sponsors, it claimed to hold its 46th annual regatta at that site in 1948. The sponsors included Harry F. McLean, famous railroad construction magnate of Merrickville, who sponsored a $1,000 Gold Cup for the 225 C.I.D. hydroplane class, and A.J. Freiman of Ottawa. I believe one of the last winners of the Freiman Trophy was Denny Arnstein of New York City and Long Island, Big Rideau Lake, the owner of New York City's Yellow Cab fleet and companion of the actress Fanny Brice, about whom the movie *Funny Girl* was made. His winning boat was a 26-foot 1937 Gar Wood called *Wag* or *Portland Wag*, driven by Carl Polk of Portland. That boat sank in Rideau Lake in about 1970 after losing a plank in rough water at high speed. The 1948 winner of the Harry McLean Gold Cup was Murray Billings of Brockville.

Some other contenders of that era who I remember include: "Bud" Wiser of Prescott, original home of Wiser's distillery and John Labatt's brewery; the Bresee family of Syracuse, N.Y., and Rideau Lake, and their *very* fast 28-foot Chris Smith (Chris-Craft) *Let's Go*; Austin Crate of Smiths Falls, who is still the owner of *Felix*, a 1937 17-foot Jeffrey build in Athens, Ontario; and the Wisemans of Rideau Lake, with their *Golden Girl*, another Jeffrey. Prominent outboard contenders were Jack Weston and Bob Allen of Smiths Falls. Slightly more recent but extremely successful competitors were Peter Burchell, Doug Caber, and Jim and Frank Ramsey of Perth, and Don Johnston of Smiths Falls, who competed internationally in the *Canada* I design racers.

In 1950, I believe it was, because of failing health, my father sold the *Riot* II to a Mr. Gamble of Richmond, Ontario, and that for the time

Left to right: **Riot II** *owned by John Millar;* **Flambeau** *owned by James Potter; and,* **Akawan** *owned by David Linkletter on the Long Reach section of the Rideau near Manotick.* – Frank Phelan

being ended my involvement with mahogany boats, but they were never forgotten! Life went on, my family purchased a cottage on Mississippi Lake near Carleton Place, where I commanded a 14-foot pine rowboat with a 5hp Johnson outboard.

In 1965, after entering into the family milk transport business, I received a call from an old friend in Merrickville, Bill Watson, who owned a marina. He had found *Riot* II, which was in pretty bad shape, and had been using it for a work boat. At that time it had a bar stool for a seat and a plywood engine cover. Syd Herwig and I went to inspect her, and we all agreed (after a thorough inspection) that $100 was a fair price for a vessel in such pristine condition! With Syd's help I then began to restore *Riot* II.

That was the beginning of Millar-Potter Restorations Limited, now a thriving business — which means I can get everybody else's boat fixed but my own. In 1965, when fibreglass boats were so popular, there were only three or four mahogany speedboats on the Long Reach. By 1975 the interest in wooden boats had increased to a point where the Manotick Classic Boat Club was formed, later becoming a chapter of an international society with over 3,100 members and some 10,000 boats. Once again, through the MCBC Antique Boat Shows, we are drawing thousands of spectators to Rideau Ferry, Ottawa and Perth, and my partner, John Millar and I, and our staff, are experiencing the invaluable satisfaction of getting many of these old boats back in service again, after they have been in storage for so many years.

Top left: "... the way we find them." A 1931 Chris Craft (24 foot) under restoration by D.J. Charles in 1988.

Top right: Peter Aikenhead fitting a plank at Millar-Potter Restorations Ltd. in 1985.

Bottom left: From left to right at the table: Blair Cook, Syd Herwig and Murray Gould look over items at Millar-Potter Restorations Ltd. in Manotick.

Bottom right. Talking boats at a Manotick Classic Boat Club workshop.

Annual workshops run by Manotick Classic Boat Club at the Millar-Potter Restorations Ltd. boatworks sustain an ongoing interest in restoration technology and new methods in wooden boat maintenance.

MARY HERWIG & FRANK PHELAN
THE MANOTICK CLASSIC BOAT CLUB

It was in January 1976 that the Manotick Classic Boat Club (MCBC) officially came into existence. None of the founding members could possibly have imagined to what proportions the movement would grow by 1988. Antique and classic boating has come into its own in North America. Fine watercraft built by past generations of boatbuilders are being ferreted out of old boathouses, barns and garages, and are being restored by loving hands to their former glory.

The Manotick club is devoted to the restoration and preservation of classic and antique boats that tell us of an era in boating that was refined and genteel, as well as exciting, fast and challenging. This is a hobby for true enthusiasts only. Classic boaters are absolute purists when it comes to originality and authenticity. No effort or expense is too great to achieve the standards of perfection necessary.

At first, MCBC was for the most part a social group for people who had some interest in early wooden boats. As the boat owners gained knowledge their activities gained momentum. They shared their knowledge generously and went about gathering more. Original wood finishing methods and authentic outfitting became the hallmark of boats owned by club members.

By a remarkable coincidence, at about the same time that this was happening at Manotick, a group was getting together at Lake George, New York. They adopted as their name "The Antique and Classic Boat Society Inc." (ACBS) and went on to establish themselves as an international organization. The Manotick Classic Boat Club was the first Canadian chapter of the ACBS, and the ACBS has grown to 32 chapters with over 3,100 members throughout North America. Manotick was also instrumental in bringing the Toronto Classic Boat Club in as the second Canadian chapter. Indeed, for a short time, Toronto and Manotick shared the MCBC newsletter, *The Brass Binnacle*. Toronto has since grown to be one of the largest clubs in North America.

James C. Potter of Manotick was the first president. Robert "Boat" Bramwell of Mahogany Harbour, Manotick, was vice-president, while Helen Ventura was elected as secretary and Linda Potter (the wife of James) was elected treasurer. Tony Layng became the social convenor.

Peter Elliott of Nepean was the first Boat Show chairman. In 1976 this show, called the "Bytown International Classic Boat Show," took place on Dows Lake, Ottawa, at the old Dows Lake Boat House, since torn down and replaced by a very modern functional structure. Forty-three boats entered, and they were of all types, sizes and shapes, and in various stages of repair. Many desperately needed careful restoration, but antiques and classics they undoubtedly were.

In 1977 the name of the show was changed to "Ottawa Classic Boat Show," and it was once again organized by Peter Elliot, under the presidency of James Potter. Jim Ventura became vice-president, Helen Ventura remained secretary, and James Millar became treasurer. Linda Potter became social convenor, a role that she continues to perform for special events to this day.

It was in 1977 that discussions began for becoming a chapter of the ACBS. The next year James Potter stepped down from the president's position and was replaced by his wife, Linda. Her superb organizational abilities and consistent application are today, as from founding days, reflected in the smooth operations of the MCBC. James went on to become the first Canadian director of the ACBS, and was shortly after joined by the second Canadian director, also from the MCBC, founding member Frank Phelan.

Howard Poole joined with Kent Martin and Robert Merkley to organize our second show, once again held at Dow's Lake. Peter Elliott turned his considerable energies to commencing our club newsletter, *The Brass Binnacle*, which has continued to this day, providing an important means of communication between our members and other ACBS chapters.

Members of the Manotick Classic Boat Club have shown boats in several international events. From left to right: Marlene Thomas, Lois Cleland, Linda Potter and Mary Herwig cook up some seafood at the Mariner's Museum, Williamsburg, Virginia, 1983.

For the years 1979, 1980 and 1981 Edgar Hendee was president. Ed's three-year presidency was a period of expansion and prosperity for the MCBC. Ed and his executives led the club to several fundraising excursions, including the MCBC Loveboat Lotteries and several small boat raffles. His 1979 executive consisted of John Ryde, vice-president, Robert Merkley, treasurer, and Dianne Elliott, secretary. This would be the second of four terms that Diane would serve in this office. In recognition of this, and hundreds of hours on various committees, Diane was awarded the prestigious President's Cup in 1987. In 1979 Kent Martin, Robert Merkley, Barbara Hopper and Frank Phelan co-chaired the last of the early Dows Lake shows.

Though the boat show changed its name to the "Ottawa International Classic Boat Show," the voluntary nature of activities did not change. As always a volunteer chairman and committee ran the show. In 1980 president Ed Hendee and his show chairman, Murray Gould (also 1980 vice-president), changed the locale of our annual event to the Rideau Ferry Inn on Big Rideau Lake. This turned out to be a great idea. The boaters loved the big expanse of water to play on, and the viewing public came in droves. They seemed to enjoy the show as much as did the boaters. On September 23, 1980, after this great success, the club decided to change the name of the boat shgow once more, and it became the "Ottawa International Antique and Classic Boat Show," and that is the name that has been used ever since.

In 1979 Ron Bradette became treasurer and his wife, Melita, became editor of *The Brass Binnacle*. Sarah Gould continued as graphic artist for the newsletter and teamed up with Frank Phelan to produce the first of three annual yearbooks, for 1980, 1981 and 1982. In 1984 Sarah received the President's Cup in recognition of her talent and efforts, which are to be seen in many MCBC publications and posters.

In 1981 membership was growing. Ed Hendee was re-elected as president, Murray Gould as vice-president, Dianne Elliott continued as secretary, and Syd Herwig was elected treasurer. Murray Gould and Ed Hendee formed a show committee of Judy Orloff, Sarah Gould, Frank Phelan, Kent Martin, and Ron Bradette to produce a second highly successful show at Rideau Ferry. Founding member John Millar co-ordinated the logistics, docking and harbour master duties for this show and several shows after.

In the spring of 1981, with months of preparation already completed, past president Linda Potter, and Nancy Taylor, proposed to the International Antique and Classic Boat Society Inc. that their annual meeting be hosted by the MCBC. This proposal was accepted, and from November 13 to 15, 1981, members of various chapters throughout North America met at the historic Chateau Montebello, in Montebello, Quebec. It was the first time the ACBS had held their annual meeting away from their Lake George base in New York, and it was an unqualified success. This endeavour by Linda

During 150th anniversary celebrations on the Rideau Canal in 1982, "Col. By" of the Royal Engineers and his wife "Esther" are conveyed to Rideau Ferry, the site of the 1982 boat show, on board **Corsair**, a 1939, 35 foot Herreshoff launch owned by James and Toni Lewis, of Vero Beach, Florida.

Potter and Nancy Taylor would later be recognized as having changed the international society's perspective, as today not only does the annual meeting move about North America, but so do the quarterly international board of directors meetings.

In 1981, the year that the club decided to seek incorporation, plans were made and approved for the MCBC to host the Antique Gold Cup Regatta at our 1982 boat show. For this important year, the 150th anniversary of the Rideau Canal, Frank Phelan was elected president, Murray Gould vice-president, Nancy Taylor secretary, and Syd Herwig treasurer. Four chairmen, Frank Phelan, Peter Elliot, Murray Gould and Robert Merkley, joined forces to organize the show, with a committee of 22 members. Their efforts were rewarded with a resounding success. The winter 1982 issue of The Brass Binnacle, tells the story:

> The show, a premier event of the many 150th anniversary celebrations on the Rideau Canal in 1982, was held at scenic Rideau Ferry, Ontario, from Friday August 13th to Sunday August 15th. One hundred and five boats were officially registered, plus sixteen antique Gold Cup racers. This was the largest assemblage of these boats in the history of the Antique Gold Cup Regatta, and the first time the regatta has been held outside the U.S. The remainder were pleasure boats of primarily runabout and cruiser design, as well as steamboats, canoes, sailboats, and outboard combinations, including several shore displays.

According to the newspapers of the day, a conservative estimate of the crowds attending over the three-day period was 20,000, reminiscent of the crowds at similar shows in the twenties and thirties. This was undoubtedly one of the finest boat shows the Manotick Classic Boat Club has put on.

In 1983 a new president, Syd Herwig, was elected. Blair Cooke was elected vice-president, Tisha Burns secretary and Ron Bradette treasurer. Later in the year Blair Cooke resigned and Murray Gould again became vice-president. Murray also chaired the boat show at Rideau Ferry and the MCBC became one of the first chapters to use the new ACBS standardized judging format. As well, Murray chaired the judging and classification committee as a Canadian director of the ACBS. Later that year the club was incorporated. Letters patent were received on December 5.

Following the great success of 1982 and an excellent follow-up show in 1983, the new board of directors felt very strongly that another change of locale was needed for the 1984 show. After much investigation of sites that had been offered, the club decided on the historic town of Perth, Ontario. Perth was regarded as the cultural centre of eastern Ontario in the early history of the province, and in 1984, when the province celebrated the 150th anniversary of the Tay Canal, we were privileged to be part of their celebrations.

Boat Show scene at the Manotick Class Boat Club's 7th Annual Ottawa International Antique and Classic Boat Show, Rideau Ferry, 1982. Held during 150th anniversary of the Rideau Canal. - Fred Hill

***Mowitza II**, Antique Boat of the Year in the 1982 Ottawa International Antique and Classic Boat Show. It is a Muskoka built Ditchburn Viking launch, then owned by Lois and Bill Cleland.* – Fred Hill

Past Manotick Classic Boat Club President Frank Phelan driving **Bonest II**, a sleek Italian-made Risa Aristron; owned by Laura Thomas.

Ed Hendee, President of the Manotick Classic Boat Club, 1979-81, in a little outboard.

Dolphine IV, 170-mph replica of Horace E. Dodge's 1932 Gold Cup Winner. Driven by owner and builder William J. Morgan of Silver Bay, New York and accompanied by Mary Jane Thomas and Wendy Hatley.

Runabouts at the Rideau Ferry Boat Show.

Donald Thomas and Murray Gould co-chaired the 1984 show. It was with pride that the club learned that 70 percent of the MCBC judging committee's recommendations had been accepted by the ACBS board of directors. The rules and the format for boat shows used in 1984 and after thus reflected in large part the standards established by the MCBC judging committee chaired by Marlene Thomas. For her many hours of research and development, establishing a co-ordinated awards program, Marlene's dedication would later be rewarded with the 1985 President's Cup. Marlene did not stop at that. She went on to organize the MCBC heritage committee, which is responsible for such projects as this book and the Cam Graham–Frank Phelan "Ten-Year Slide History of the MCBC." The Perth show was a great success.

The club's annual meeting in November 1984 was conducted to conform with our new letters patent, so that 12 new directors were elected. These directors elected the officers of the club at their first meeting. Syd Herwig was returned as president, Linda Potter was elected vice-president, Ron Bradette treasurer and Mary Herwig secretary. Murray Gould, once again, was chairman for the boat show in 1985, again at Rideau Ferry.

In 1986 the new board elected Mary Herwig president, Linda Potter vice-president, Frank Milotte treasurer and Alan MacLeod secretary. Syd Herwig and Murray Gould were chairmen for the 1986 show. The show returned to Dows Lake, where it all began, only this time the show was held at the new Dows Lake Pavilion in Ottawa. It was a tremendous success. Class boat races were initiated for the first time, to the delight of entrants and spectators alike. Founding president James Potter was presented the President's Cup for years of promotion and loyalty to the club. In November 1986, at the annual meeting, the new board elected Alan MacLeod president, Mel Evans vice-president, Dinah Scholfield secretary and Frank Milotte treasurer. Syd Herwig consented to chair the 1987 show, which took place once again at Dows Lake, and again featured boat races. The finale of the races saw six beautiful mahogany boats riding abreast down Dow's Lake, full speed to the finish line. It was a beautiful sight to behold and a thrill to all present.

The ACBS annual meeting returned to Canada for 1987. For their outstanding efforts and dedication to antique and classic boating, for having both served as presidents of their club, for having edited and published their club newsletters and other work, Mary and Syd Herwig were the first Canadians to be presented the highest award of the ACBS, the Founder's Award.

As this is written the club begins its twelfth full year of existence. it has grown from humble beginnings to a remarkable collection of fine boats and proud owners. Of the 23 founding members, eight are still active. They include: James Potter and his partner in the Millar-Potter Boat Restoration Company, John Millar; John's brother, Jim Millar, partner in the Manotick Marina; Linda Potter; Frank Phelan; Peter and Diane Elliot; and Dave Linkletter. Under the

Prize winners at the 9th annual Ottawa International Antique and Classic Boat Show held in Perth in 1984 as part of the "Haggart's Ditch" celebration to mark the 150th anniversary of the Tay Canal. - Frank Phelan

presidency of Alan Macleod, re-elected in 1988, along with Mel Evans and Dinah Scholfield as vice-president and secretary, and with a new treasurer, John Ritchie, the Manotick Classic Boat Club is in prime condition to keep going for many years to come. About 90 classic boats, some of them of exceptional beauty and worth, are now registered to owners in the club. More are waiting to be found by boat lovers, classic boats tucked away or hidden, abandoned or lost. They and their owners will always find good company at Manotick.

Manotick, as described in the second chapter of this book, is a small town near Ottawa on the Rideau, but it is known through the activities of the MCBC from coast to coast in North America. Indeed, some classic and antique boat owners would say that Ottawa is a large city near Manotick.

By the time this book is printed the 1988 boat show, chaired by Graeme Beattie and Mel Evans at Rideau Ferry, will be history. To those of us who see the beauty of our classic watercraft, and admire the workmanship of the people who make such works of art out of good wood and equipment of good quality, it is a comfort to know that we can preserve something of the values and pleasures that they represent. We hope that others share something of that feeling.

Manotick Classic Boat Show judges at Rideau Ferry in 1985. The judges carefully evaluate all entries in determining prize winners.

APPENDICES

PHOTOGRAPHS
(in no particular order)

REGISTER OF MCBC CLASSIC & ANTIQUE BOATS
(alphabetically by owner)

SYD & MARY HERWIG'S *CALYPSO*

Syd Herwig bought this 1924 Dodge watercar from Alf Boyd. Carvel-built of mahogany on white oak, it is fitted with a Chrysler 318 marine engine.

1982 CRAFTSMANSHIP AWARD (CLAYTON)
1983 & 1985 BEST ANTIQUE RUNABOUT (MCBC)
1987 PARTICIPANTS' CHOICE (LAKE CHAMPLAIN)
1987 ANTIQUE BOAT OF THE YEAR (MCBC)

JAMES C. POTTER'S *JIM'S JAM*
A 1941 Chris-Craft runabout, this boat was bought by James Potter in poor condition at Jamestown, New York, in 1977 and restored extensively on spec for a customer who did not materialize, hence the name.
1983 BEST UTILITY (MCBC)

MURRAY & SARAH GOULD'S **WARPATH**
 A 1927 *decked-in, carvel-built, mahogany-on-oak Chris-Craft runabout fitted with a 1927 Kermath 100 hp 6-cylinder engine.*
1983 ANTIQUE BOAT OF THE YEAR (MCBC)

DOUG & NANCY PORTER'S ***RAZZ MA TAZZ***
A 1955 *Shepherd runabout, oak and mahogany.*
1984 BEST BOAT ON THE RIDEAU LAKES (MCBC)
1984 & 1986 CLASSIC BOAT OF THE YEAR (MCBC)
1986 BEST CANADIAN BUILT BOAT (MCBC)
1988 BEST ENGINE COMPARTMENT (MCBC)

RON BRADETTE'S *CASPER*
One of a kind, a 1905 Chestnut motorized canoe. Built by Chestnut Canoe of Fredericton, New Brunswick, it is fitted with a 1904 Roberts 2-cylinder, 6 hp engine built in Charlottetown, P.E.I.

1981 & 1982 PEOPLE'S CHOICE (MCBC)
1983 BEST CANOE (MCBC)
1984 BEST ANTIQUE CANOE (MCBC)

ADRIAN N. RICHMOND'S **MISS LITTLEHAMPTON**

This Burleigh-model rowing skiff built by Peterborough Canoe about 1950 was originally bought by Camp Oconto, described by the present owner as a high-class camp for girls. The next owner drilled a hole through the keel in order to install an inboard engine, then stored the boat in a workshop. Adrian Richmond acquired it in 1986 and is restoring it. There is a walnut strip three inches below the top of the gunwhale, otherwise it is cedar strip on ash ribs, with an oak keel and pine seats.

MRS. TONY LEWIS' *RIOT*

Built in 1950 "to beat neighbours' boats on Minnesota Lake, and did," this Class E service runabout by Davis Brothers of Manteo, North Carolina, is made of marine plywood. It was laid up in a barn until 1985, and given to the present owner as a Christmas present after being restored in 18 days.

1987 CLASSIC BOAT OF THE YEAR (MCBC)

J.P. LEWIS' **CORSAIR**
This Herreshoff yacht launch was built in 1939 as the starboard launch for J.P. Morgan's **Corsair IV**. She was not put on board during the Second World War and was acquired by the former owner instead. (**Corsair**'s boat show awards are too numerous to list.)

DON & MARLENE THOMAS'
LADY GILBERT
   An exceptionally fine example of the work of the Gilbert yard in Brockville, this launch was built about 1920. It is believed to have been shipped to Point-au-Baril by flatcar, used by the Oldfields during the summer, possibly to move goods from the train station to their island, and stored in Thornbury, Ontario, during the winter. It was in Thornbury that the Thomases bought the launch from Matt Kloos, who they think owned it for 35 to 40 years. The boat was restored in 1986-87 by Millar-Potter Restorations.
1987 BEST ANTIQUE LAUNCH & PEOPLES CHOICE (MCBC)
1988 BEST LAUNCH (BISCAYNE, FLORIDA)
1988 PEOPLES CHOICE (MT. DORA, FLORIDA)

FRANK PHELAN'S ***LILLIAN T. II***
Used by the Fleishmann and Layng families on Charleston Lake from 1924 to 1972, it was identified by the Layngs as a Gilbert, but it seems possible that this is a Peterborough autocraft for which Gilbert Marine was the distributor.
1977 BEST CANADIAN RUNABOUT (MCBC)

ALAN MACLEOD'S *LEGAL TENDER*
Millar-Potter Restorations *restored this 1953 Chris-Craft special sportsman utility runabout between 1983 and 1985; the engine was rebuilt in 1987.*
1985 BEST UTILITY (MCBC)
1986 CLASSIC BOAT OF THE YEAR, CO-WINNER (MCBC)
1988 BEST UTILITY (MCBC)

BILL, JANE & ELIZABETH MOORE'S **EL TORO**
A utility runabout built in 1954 by Greavette of Gravenhurst.
1986 LONGEST WATER VOYAGE SELF PROPELLED (MCBC)

DON & MARLENE THOMAS' **KON TIKI-TOO**
  This Shepherd runabout, purchased at the factory by Christopher T. Thomas in 1953 and transferred to Don and Marlene Thomas in 1970, was completely stripped down and refinished by Greavette in 1978-79, and has since been maintained as new by Millar-Potter Restorations.
1979 & 1982 CLASSIC BOAT OF THE YEAR (MCBC)
1982 BEST SHEPHERD & BEST COSMETIC OVERALL APPEARANCE (TORONTO CHAPTER – ACBS)
1982 & 1985 & 1986 & 1988 CLASSIC RUNABOUT (MCBC)
1983 BEST CANADIAN BUILT BOAT (MCBC)
1984 BEST SHEPHERD & BEST CANADIAN BUILT BOAT (CAN-AM GANANOQUE)
1985 BEST BOAT ON THE RIDEAU LAKES (MCBC)

DAVE LINKLETTER'S *YNYESCRAIG*

Acquired by Dave Linkletter in 1979, the distinguishing characteristic of this 1920 W.J. Malette launch are its sliding hatch and fold-down windshield attached to the hatch.

1980 BEST CANADIAN BOAT (CLAYTON)
1981 BEST LAUNCH (MCBC)
1981 BEST CRAFTSMANSHIP AWARD (CLAYTON)
1983 PROFESSIONAL CRAFTSMANSHIP (MCBC)

GRAEME BEATTIE'S **SPIRIT OF ST. ANNE**
   A 1950 Chris-Craft, this carvel-built mahogany runabout belonged to the first vice-president of the MCBC, Bob Bramwell.
1984 BEST CLASSIC RUNABOUT (MCBC)
1986 BEST CHRIS-CRAFT (TORONTO)
1986 & 1988 BEST BOAT ON THE RIDEAU LAKES (MCBC)

TOM & PAM LAZIO'S **POKETANYA**

This 1933 Elco cruiser has a long and varied history. The second owner, Mr. Dilcer of Rochester, derived the name from his wife's nickname, "Poke," and the Hungarian word "tanya" which means "house of spiders." In the 1960s it was the training vessel for a troop of Sea Scouts.

1977 BEST CRUISER & ANTIQUE BOAT OF THE YEAR (CLAYTON)
1978 BEST AMERICAN CRUISER (MCBC)
1980 & 1983 BEST CRUISER (CLAYTON)
1981 BEST CRUISER (MCBC)
1983 BEST POWERBOAT (MYSTIC RENDEZVOUS)

CAMERON & JOCELYN GRAHAM'S **L'AVENTURE**

Built at Platt's Eyeot, Hampton, England, in 1933 for Thames Estuary cruising, designed and built by John I. Thornycroft and Sons, it was Boat of the Show at the London International Boat show of 1933. Woods used in construction include African and Honduras mahogany, teak, English oak, and rock elm. It has copper rivets throughout. The bottom is single ⅞" mahogany planking, the transom is slightly curved, and there is a mast for a steadying foresail on the foredeck. The fittings are 80% original. Requisitioned in the Second World War for the Royal Army Service Corps, it was one of the "Little Ships of Dunkirk." Acquired by General Jean Victor Allard of the Canadian army in 1962, she was brought to Canada and sold to John Flanders in 1965, and he in turn sold her to Cameron and Jocelyn Graham of Manotick in 1966.

1933 BOAT OF THE SHOW (LONDON INTERNATIONAL BOAT SHOW, U.K.)
1974 CRAFTSMANSHIP AWARD (CLAYTON)
1976 & 1985 BEST CRUISER (CLAYTON)
1976 BEST CRUISER (MCBC)
1978 BEST CANADIAN CRUISER (CLAYTON)
1984 MOST HISTORIC BOAT (MCBC)
1986 & 1987 BEST ANTIQUE CRUISER (MCBC)

JIM & TONY LEWIS' *MAVOURNEEN*

This magnificent 50-foot launch is one of four yacht tenders built in 1930 by Camper-Nicholson of Gosport, England, including one owned by Peter de Savory, one of the English challengers for the Americas' Cup in 1980. It was three years in restoration at Hurley-on-Thames, England, before being shipped to Fort Lauderdale, Florida, in a container.

1988 BEST OF SHOW (BISCAYNE, FLORIDA)
1988 PEOPLES CHOICE & BEST ANTIQUE LAUNCH (MCBC)

RON LANG'S **WILL-O-THE-WISP**

    This is a 1934 Earl Barnes decked-in, carvel-built runabout with a 1947 Ford-Offenhauser 225 hp engine.

1936 WINNER OF CLASS IN RACES AT CANADIAN NATIONAL EXHIBITION
1983 PEOPLE'S CHOICE (MCBC)

GEORGE DRUMMOND'S *LONG SAULT*

From 1949-1951 the **Long Sault** worked on the Richelieu Canal, then on the Rideau system till 1975. It was mothballed at Beveridge's Lock till it sold in the fall of 1979.

1981 BEST WORK BOAT; 1983 BEST UTILITY; 1985 BEST COMMERCIAL CLASS; 1986 LONGEST WATER VOYAGE (MCBC)

CARMEN KEYS' **MISS JANE**
Port Carling Boatworks produced this 1936 mahogany runabout. It is fitted with a 1936 Lycoming 45 hp engine.
1979 BEST ANTIQUE RUNABOUT (MCBC)

PETER & TOOTS BURCHELL'S *RIDEAU SPRAY II*

Wendall Browne built this 42-foot displacement cruiser, with its high freeboard and offshore trawler design, at his home on Briton Bay, Big Rideau Lake. Launched in 1979, it was finally completed in 1987, after being purchased by Peter Burchell of Perth in 1986. It has a double-berth cabin, wood stove and copper-plate chimney.

1987 BEST BOAT ON THE RIDEAU LAKES & BEST CONTEMPORARY CRUISER (MCBC)

MEL & PEARL EVANS' **OLD SMOOTHIE**

Myles Jeffrey custom built this runabout in 1938 for Alfred and Ethel Lang of Smiths Falls, for use at their Lower Rideau Lake cottage. Alfred Lang is said never to have allowed the boat to be driven at over 1500 rpm, and always with one hatch door open. He used the boat every summer until he was 90 years of age, and left it in his stone boathouse until his death at 97. Purchased with the cottage in 1976, it was restored by Millar-Potter Restorations in 1978. The EE registration was given when Smiths Falls was designated an outport of Ottawa. The 157th to be licensed under the new laws, she still proudly flies the Union Jack.
1984 BEST ANTIQUE RUNABOUT (MCBC)

ROBERT O. BALL'S *ZEPHYR*

This 1954 Peterborough carvel-built cedar-strip outboard was exchanged by its original owner for garden equipment at a Goderich dealer about 1981. Mr. Doug Splan bought the boat and revarnished it in 1985. Since that date nothing has been done to it, but it won two awards at the 1987 MCBC boat show.

1987 BEST BOAT/MOTOR COMBINATION (MCBC)
1987 BEST BIG IRON (MCBC)

AL & BEV MCKENNEY'S
OLYVE-ED
   Purchased by Ed McKenney for family use in 1930, this Dowsett power skiff has always been kept on the Rideau Lakes.
1986 BEST POWER SKIFF (CLAYTON)

JOHN D. RICHARDS' *LYNDA IV*

The Chris-Craft 33-foot cruiser for 1939, the boat is said to have been launched in August of that year, hauled out of the water at the end of the season, kept on blocks under cover until 1944, and launched again in 1945. The second owner, in 1951, took the boat to Toronto, and the third, in 1962, sailed it on Lake Simcoe. It is now based at Poonamalie Landing during the summer season.

LOUIS & MICHELE MARTINEAU'S **CHIMERE**

One of the best-known boats on the Rideau system, beautifully fitted out, this 1946 Chris-Craft cruiser has travelled to New York City by way of Lake Champlain and the Hudson River, through the barge canal to Oswego and on to Niagara Falls and Toronto, up the Trent-Severn system to Georgian Bay, and in 1984 to Quebec to greet the "Tall Ships."

1981 BEST CANADIAN CRUISER (CLAYTON)
1983 BEST CLASSIC CRUISER (MCBC)
1984 CHRIS-CRAFT AWARD (MCBC)

DAVID GOWING'S **TEREK**

Kept for years at Oakville by F.M. Rickey, this Rickey Brothers sailboat was acquired by A.G.S. Sandison of Rideau Ferry and renamed **Terek** after the Russian bird of that name, a sandpiper indigenous to northeastern Europe, the Sandison ancestral home. She has sailed through the Thousand Islands many times, went up the Trent Canal in the 1940s, crossed Lake Ontario to Youngstown dock and has sailed down the St. Lawrence as far as Montreal.
1978 & 1980 & 1982 & 1984 & 1986 & 1988 BEST SAILBOAT AWARD (MCBC)

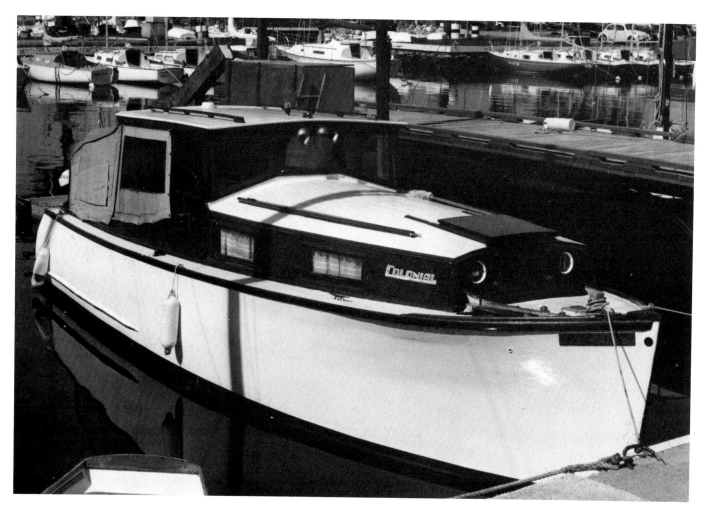

BYRON & DUSTY WOOD'S *DIXIE BELLE*

This 1929 Colonial BW displacement cruiser was a charter fishing boat on Chesapeake Bay for 35 years, then purchased in 1966 by Major Joe Liesse, USAF, who brought the boat to Portland. It was bought by the Woods in 1970. The name indicates the boat used to be kept south of the Mason-Dixon line.

J.P. LEWIS' **YESTERDAY**
  Originally named **This**, **Yesterday** is number 3 of 20 racing launches built by Leyare as a racing class for the Thousand Islands Yacht Club, believed to be the first one-design racing class in North America. Built in 1910 for George C. Boldt.
1985 HISTORIC BOAT OF THE YEAR (MUSKOKA)
1985 HISTORIC BOAT OF THE YEAR (MCBC)

CAROL SIMPSON & DOUG WILLIAMS' ***THE LAUNCH***

Built in about 1910 by the Chestnut Canoe Company, this boat has been in the Simpson family since 1919, has had two full lives and is beginning another. Benjamin Roy Simpson bought her from Mr. Stevens of the Dennis Canadian Lumber Company in 1919, and he said, "Her engine never missed a beat from 1919 to 1942." After the Second World War, during which family vacations were put on hold, Benjamin's son Roy retrieved the boat from under the water in the boathouse at Whitney, and in 1953 the engine was made to work again, but in 1961 the boat went into storage. in 1983 Carol Simpson and her husband, Doug Williams, took the boat out of storage and found Ted Moores and Joan Barrett of the Bear Mountain Boat Shop, who were able to restore the boat.

1985 BEST POWERED SKIFF

BRIAN & LESLEY KIRK'S **SAGITTA**
Ed Hendee purchased this 1934 Greavette in the late 1970s, in very poor condition. Millar-Potter restored the boat completely in 1982.

ROBERT MERKLEY'S **MARION**
Cam Merkley bought this 1965 Shepherd runabout with the money his wife, Marion, had saved to refurnish the living room, hence the name. Harry Belafonte is said to have gone waterskiing with this boat in 1963.
1977 BEST SHEPHERD (MCBC)

DAVID GRAY'S *5738*

This unnamed, fast 1938 Peterborough rowing skiff was purchased in 1955 at Juniper Boat Works, Stoney Lake, and won races in several Stoney Lake regattas. In 1980 the boat was rotting, and the Tottenham family decided to burn it. The Gray family rescued it, had it restored by Millar-Potter Restorations and presented it to David Gray as a surprise for his 40th birthday.

BILL, JANE & ELIZABETH MOORE'S ***RIDEAU PASSAGE***

Built in Smiths Falls by Davy Nichol, this launch was used every weekend in the 1930s for travel from Smiths Falls to Erora Lodge on Big Rideau Lake.

1982 BEST BOAT ON THE RIDEAU LAKES (MCBC)
1983 BEST HISTORIC RUNABOUT (MCBC)

CAROLINE EVANS' *THE CEDAR CANOE*
This is one of the original Peterborough wide-board canoes designed to be sailed as well as paddled. The original sails are being restored. The canoe was purchased about 1906 by Caroline's father, and the family has had it ever since. The sail has been replaced, but the spars are original. It has always been called **The Cedar Canoe** and has been in more or less continual use. The lee boards are not the originals but are of the same vintage.
1987 & 1988 BEST WOODEN CANOE (MCBC)

ANN & MICHAEL MATHESON'S **TRADITION**

The Matheson's brought this 1929 Chris-Craft Commuter from Miami for the 1984 MCBC show at Perth, Ontario, and won four awards. The boat cruises at 20 knots, has a top speed of 32 knots, and uses about 10 gallons of fuel an hour. The Mathesons bought the boat from a boat yard in Long Island in 1980 and restored her piece by piece to her original state.

1984 BEST CHRIS-CRAFT CRUISER (MCBC)
1984 BEST ANTIQUE CRUISER (MCBC)
1984 PEOPLES CHOICE (MCBC)

VICKI & JOHN RITCHIE'S **SPINDRIFT**

This is a well-documented example of the "standarized runabout-utility model" Ditchburn, of which 123 were built at Gravenhurst between 1925 and 1928. Used in Georgian Bay, it was kept at Pointe au Baril, at Richardson's Boat Livery, now known as the Beacon Marina. When the boat changed owners in 1939, the "rather lazy" 4-cylinder engine was replaced with a Buchanan 6-cylinder Rocket 85. Since then it has changed owners several times, being moved to Dunnville, Ontario about 1960, and kept in storage in a barn from 1973 to 1978. It was put in the water again, in Georgian Bay, by Bob Berry, then placed in storage at Thompson's Marine until Berry sold it to John P. Ritchie. In September 1981 it was moved, "with the much appreciated assistance of MCBC members," to Manotick, and was restored by Millar-Potter Restorations in 1986.

DAVID & DINAH SCHOLFIELD'S **M'LORA**

In 1949 Grew Boats Ltd. of Penetanguishene, Ontario, built this Admiral and sold it under the name **Truant** to a customer on Georgian Bay. Six months later it caught fire and nearly sank, and on the advice of the insurance company was written off. The men who had extinguished the fire then repaired the boat. The next owner enjoyed the boat for over 15 years, but it had some rough experiences. James Potter came upon the vessel at the Duke marina in Port Carling and acquired it for his summer home on Big Rideau Lake, but in September 1983 David Scholfield saw it lying in the yard at Millar-Potter Restorations and acquired it himself. After four years of painstaking restoration, finished off by Millar-Potter, the boat was launched in June 1987.

1987 BEST UTILITY (MCBC)
1988 CLASSIC BOAT OF THE YEAR (MCBC)

AT JULY, 1988
REGISTER OF MCBC BOATS

Peter & Barb Aikenhead
LITTLE CROW
Ottawa
    1933 Chris-Craft, carvel-planked white oak & mahogany, twin cockpit runabout. LOA 18', LWL 17'6", beam 5'4", draft 10", fitted with Chris-Craft 90 hp engine, curved light tumblehome transom.

Robert O. Ball
ZEPHYR 16E167
Goderich, Ont. & Minden, Ont.
Previous owner: Douglas Splan, Clinton, Ont.
    1954 Peterborough cedar-strip carvel-built, LOA 14', draft 20", beam 50", with 1954 Evinrude 15 hp Fastwin outboard, oak transom, original fittings. 1987 Best Boat/Motor Combination (MCBC), 1987 Best Big Iron (MCBC).

Graeme Beattie
SPIRIT OF STE ANNE 74E519
Rideau Ferry, Ont.
Previous owners: J.J. Day & Bob Bramwell
    1950 Chris-Craft decked runabout, carvel-built mahogany on oak, LOA 20', LWL 19'6", beam 6', draft 1', 1950 Hercules CC conversion, 158 hp. Built Algonac, Michigan. Boat show awards: 1984 Classic runabout (MCBC), 1986 Best Chris-Craft (Toronto), 1986 & 1988 Best Boat on the Rideau Lakes (MCBC).

John & Gayl Bignell
HEIDI
Ottawa, Ont.
Previous owners: Tom Ritchie & John Ritchie
    1957 Burgland outboard with deck, LOA 15', LWL 14'5", beam 5'4"; 1957 Johnston, 35 hp. Built Willington, Illinois. Has original canvas cover and original decals.

Ron Bradette
CASPER
Manotick, Ont.
3 previous owners
    1905 Chestnut motorized canoe, LOA 18½', LWL 18½', beam 3', draft 10", 1904 Roberts 2-cylinder, 6 hp. Built Charlottetown, PEI, cedar-strip, canvas-covered, canvas canopy, custom-built, one-of-a-kind with sponsons. Modified by Chestnut. Boat show awards: 1981 People's Choice (MCBC), 1982 Peoples Choice (MCBC), 1983 Best Canoe (MCBC), 1984 Antique Canoe (Ottawa).

James F. Brennan
SHADY LADY NY 3510-EC
Syracuse, NY.
Previous owners: Kate Smith, Joseph Esposito, Gary Cope
Previous names: Sunshine One, Ruthie
    1929 Chris-Craft runabout designed by Chris Smith, LOA 26', LWL 26', beam 6'8", draft 24", 1929 Chris-Craft engine, built Algonac, Michigan, of Honduras mahogany. Boat show awards: 1984 Antique Boat of the Year & Chris-Craft runabout (MCBC), 1985 Runabout runner-up (Thousand Islands), 1985 Best Antique Boat (Finger Lakes, NY), 1985 2nd place in Hammondsport – Penn Yan race.

Gary Bryson
Unnamed 60E-9144
Bracebridge, Ont. & Hay Bay, Bay of Quinte
Previous owners: Jack Vanderhout 1960-71, Lake Simcoe; Sid Freedman, 1971-87, Lake of Bays

A 1960 Shepherd mahogany model 110 V-drive runabout with the original Chrysler 318 cu. in. engine, LOA 22', beam 22', draft 3', padded side panels.

Peter and Toots Burchell
RIDEAU SPRAY II
Kingston, Ont. & Portland, Ont.
Previous owner: W. Browne

Displacement cruiser commissioned in 1979, designed and built by W. Browne of Briton Bay, near Portland, Ont. Carvel-built of oak, mahogany, pine, cherry and butternut, LOA 42', LWL 38', beam 13'8", draft 4', fitted with 1977 390 cu. in. Ford diesel engine. Awards: 1987 Best Boat on the Rideau Lakes and Best Contemporary Cruiser (MCBC).

Donald Joseph Charles
Unnamed 35E 946
Parry Sound, Ont. & Orillia, Ont.

1930 Chris-Craft utility, LOA 24', beam 7', draft 18", carvel-built of mahogany and oak, with 1931 125 hp Chrysler engine. Built in Algonac, Michigan.

Harold J. Cherry
Unnamed 24E 2535
London, Ont. & Ottawa, Ont.

1957 Chris-Craft runabout, LOA 17', beam 7'1", draft 2', carvel-built, mahogany, 230 cu. in. engine. Built at Cadillac, Michigan.

Lorayne E. Couch
FELIX II
Smiths Falls, Ont.
Previous owner: George Austin Crate

1938 decked two-cockpit runabout, LOA 16', beam 53", draft 2', 1938 Gray Marine Phantom, 6-cylinder, 75 hp. Boat designed and built by Myles Jeffery, Athens, Ontario. Boat show awards: 1981 Antique Runabout of the Year (MCBC)

George Drummond
LONG SAULT
Ottawa
Previous owner: Canadian Government

1949 clinker-built steel tug, LOA 45', LWL 40', beam 12'6", draft 5', 1949 Cummins (original) diesel engine, 855 cu. in. Built by Russell Bros., Owen Sound, Ont. Awards: 1981 Best Work Boat, 1983 Best Utility, 1985 Best Commercial Class, 1986 Longest Water Voyage (MCBC).

Caroline Evans
THE CEDAR CANOE
Massawippi, Quebec

Cedar board canoe, LOA 16'. Designed and built by Wm. English, Peterborough, 1906. This is one of the original Peterborough wide-board canoes designed to be sailed as well as padled. The original sails are being restored. Awards: 1987 & 1988 Best Canoe Wood (MCBC).

Robert E. Evans
MISS EMILY 16D 901
Sherbrooke, Que. & Kanata

Outboard runabout, LOA 15', LWL 15', beam 6', 1957 Johnston, 35 hp carvel-built western red cedar and oak. Designed and built by the Canadian Canoe Company, Peterborough, 1958.

Mel & Pearl Evans
OLD SMOOTHIE 32EE157
Smiths Falls
Previous owner: Alfred Lang
Previous name: Eth-Al

> 1938 Jeffrey twin-cockpit runabout, carvel-built of oak, mahogany and butternut, LOA 20'8", beam 6', draft 1'6", fitted with 1938 Kermath 6-cylinder 237 cu. in. engine. Awards: 1984 Best Antique Runabout (MCBC).

Rod Evans
PHOENIX 50E16180
Toronto & Ottawa, Ont.
Previous owner: R.K. Wilson
Previous name: Mohawk

> 1957 outboard cedar-strip runabout. Built by Lakefield Boats of cedar, oak and mahogany. LOA 17'6", beam 3'6", draft 12", with original 1957 Johnson 35 hp engine.

Stephen Fox
CONEMARA
Rideau Ferry, Ont.
Previous owners: Derrel Seaward, 1965-1969; kept at Len's Cove 1951-1965; John Wirt, 1932-1951, Conemara Island and Smiths Falls
Previous name: First Class

> 1932 Jeffrey-decked runabout, original 75 hp Kermath engine replaced in 1960s with 100 hp Ford flathead, LOA 23', LWL 21', beam 21', draft 15", double bottom, Philippine mahogany on oak wood, stainless steel fastenings. Built by Myles Jeffrey, Athens, Ont.

Gordon & Vernie Foy
TANGMERE
Ottawa
Previous owners: Bob Moore, 1962-75; Mac Reis, 1978-83)
Previous name: Sea Wolf

> Owens Express cruiser, LOA 30', LWL 27', beam 10'9", draft 2'6", twin engines, Flagship 185 hp, 8-cylinder, 1962, port engine replaced 1979. Boat built in 1962 by Owens in Baltimore. Carvel-built of mahogany on oak.

Bruce & Florence Gaw
SEA WOLF 86E10876
Newmarket, Ont. & Johnstown Marina, Bridgeview, Ont.

> 1969 Pacemaker sedan cruiser, carvel-built of mahogany on oak, LOA 32', LWL 29'4", beam 11'4", draft 3', fitted with original 1969 350 hp Pacemaker Chevrolet engine, 327 cu. in.

David T. Gowing
TEREK 310 128
Ottawa
Previous owners: E.M Rickey, Rex Long, A.G.S. Sandison, Frances Atchison, Cdr. Tony Law, Earl Checkley, Daniel Spry
Previous name: Dolphin II

> 1937 sloop, canoe stern, LOA 22'6", beam 7'6", draft 3'6", with 1956 Buchanan midget 25 hp engine. Built in Oakville, Ont. by Rickey Bros. Awards: 1978, 1980, 1982, 1984, 1986, 1988 Best Sail Boat (MCBC).

Murray & Sarah Gould
WARPATH 74E5345
Portland, Ont. & Mahogany Harbour

    1927 Chris-Craft decked-in runabout, carvel-built, mahogany on oak, LOA 26'6", LWL 26', beam 6', draft 18", with 1927 Kermath 100 hp 6-cylinder engine, 535 cu. in. Built at Algonac, Michigan Awards: 1983 Antique Boat of the Year (MCBC).

Cameron & Jocelyn Graham
L'AVENTURE 163 458
Manotick, Ont. & London, England
Previous owners: John Flanders; General J.V. Allard, War Office, Britain; & other British owners
Previous names: Ronboy; Dragonfly; Sea Leech II

    1933 Thornycroft carvel-built cruiser, LOA 35', LWL 33'9", beam 9'1", draft 2'7", twin 20 hp Bukh diesels, 1984. Built at Hampton-on-Thames. Awards: 1974 Craftsmanship; 1976 & 1985 Best Cruiser; 1978 Best Canadian (Clayton); 1976 Best Cruiser; 1984 Most Historic; 1986 &1987 Best Antique Cruiser (MCBC).

David R. & Sally Gray
Unnamed 5738
Metcalfe, Ont.
Previous owner: Charles Tottenham, Trinity College School, Port Hope, Ont.

    Peterborough carvel-built double-ended cedar rowing skiff, circa 1938.

David & Sally Gray & family
Unnamed

    Peterborough cedar-strip canoe covered with canvas, probably built in the 1930s, adapted for rowing with iron-rod outriggers.

David Gray
Unnamed
Previous owner: Dominic Kelly

    Flat-bottomed rowing boat made for rental purposes by Dominic Kelly of Kelly's Landing, probably the last of its kind, and stored in a barn near Metcalfe, Ontario, until museum space can be found.

Syd & Mary Herwig
CALYPSO 32E-3889
Manotick, Ont.
Previous owner: Alf Boyd

    1924 Dodge planing runabout, carvel-built of mahogany on white oak, LOA 22'6", LWL 22'4", beam 6', draft 18", with 1941 Ford St. Lawrence conversion engine, 200+ cu. in. Designed by George Crouch and built by Horace Dodge of Detroit, Michigan. Awards: 1982 Craftsmanship (Clayton); 1983, 1985 Best Antique Runabout (MCBC); 1987 Participants' Choice (Lake Champlain Basin Harbor Club); 1987 Antique Boat of the Year (MCBC).

Gordon F. Howarth
LOLA PHIL II
Previous owner: Philip Clegg

    1938 triple-cockpit runabout, carvel-built of mahogany on oak by Rice Lake Boat Works, designed by Tom Wallace, LOA 26', LWL 25'6", beam 6', draft 18", with 1938 Kermath 100 hp engine. Built at Gore's Landing, Ont., structurally restored by Millar-Potter Boat Works Ltd. in 1985.

David J. Hunter
CONTENT 32 E 107
Ottawa & Charleston Lake, Ont.
Previous owner: Marshal Sherk
> 1938 Chris-Craft inboard batten-seam runabout, mahogany on white oak, LOA 17', beam 6', draft 1'5½", with 1938 Chris-Craft 95 hp engine, rebuilt 1984. Built in Algonac, Michigan, completely restored 1978-1984.

Don Johnson
Unnamed
> 1940 Peterborough outboard lakeside runabout, LOA 17'.

Don Johnson
Unnamed
> 1983 replica of a 1910 Sunnyside canoe built by Ted Moores of Bancroft, Ont., LOA 16'.

Wooden Keel Limited
Murray Gould, Al McLeod, Frank Phelan
MYRNA
Toronto & Manotick, Ont.
Previous name: Delnar
> 1937 Sachau marine cruiser, carvel-built in Toronto of mahogany, LOA 32', LWL 31'7", beam 10'5", draft 2'4", fitted with twin 1937 6-cylinder Chrysler engines, extensive chrome work.

Tom Keyes
PUFFIN
Blackburn Barn, Ont.
Previous owner: Peter Molin
> 1939 Duke clinker-built mahogany-on-oak launch, LOA 19', LWL 18'6", beam 5'6", draft 18", with 1939 Buchanan 25 hp midget engine. Built in Gravenhurst, Ont., now being restored.

Ted Keyes
STING 18 E 10739
Ottawa, Ont.
Previous name: Lobo
> 1940 Chris-Craft carvel-built special runabout, LOA 16', LWL 15'6", draft 18", with 1940 Buchanan 60 hp. Built in Algonac, Michigan. Engine found by Ed Hendee in Keswick, Ont. 1979 & restored by Keyes.

Ted Keyes
DREAM ON
Ottawa
> 1937 Chris-Craft triple-cockpit decked runabout, Honduras mahogany on oak, LOA 22', LWL 21'6", beam 6', draft 20", with 1937 Chris-Craft KLC 95 hp engine.

Carmen Keyes
MISS JANE 24 E 2654
London & Rockcliffe, Ont.
Previous owner: Stan Sibthorpe
> 1936 utility runabout, Honduras mahogany on oak, LOA 18', LWL 18', beam 5'6", draft 18", with 1936 Lycoming 45 hp engine. Built by Port Carling Boat Works. Awards: 1979 Best Antique Runabout (MCBC).

Brian & Lesley Kirk
SAGITTA
Portland & Ottawa, Ont.
Previous owner: Ed Hendee

    1934 Greavette runabout carvel-built of mahogany, LOA 18'5", beam 6', draft 18", fitted with 1955 Gray marine 75 hp engine. Boat rebuilt approx. 1982 by Millar-Potter Boat Works.

Ron Lang
BETTY LOU
Huntsville & Arnprior, Ont.

    Originally kept by C.H. Musselman of Kitchener, Ont., at his Huntsville cottage, this 1935 Barnes triple-cockpit runabout lay in a dump in Orillia for at least 20 years. It has a 1935 Chrysler Crown 125 hp engine.

Ron Lang
WILL-O-THE-WISP 60 E 88
Previous owner: T. Lang-Moffat

    1934 Earl Barnes decked-in carvel-built runabout, LOA 19'6", with 1947 Ford-Offenhauser 225 hp engine. Awards: 1936 Canadian National Exhibition races, 1st in class; 1983 People's Choice (MCBC).

Ron Lang
VALHALLA
Previous owner: *thought to have been Nelson Davis*

    1937 Earl Barnes carvel-built runabout-torpedo, LOA 23', beam 8', with 1937 gray Fireball 150 hp engine. May have been custom built for Nelson Davis in the Muskokas.

Ron Lang
SILVER DON
Previous owner: Ross Therrien

    1936 Peterborough, triple-cockpit, decked-in runabout, cedar on white oak, LOA 21', LWL 20'6", beam 6', with 1936 Buchanan 90 hp engine. Awards: 1983 People's Choice.

Thomas & Pamela Lazio
POKETANYA
Fairport, NY
Previous owners: Jacob Goldstein, Mr. & Mrs. Dilcer, Herbert Glick, Julius Schenk, Webster Kiwanis Club, David Brugger.
Previous names: Boleda, Jay Lee

    1933 carvel-built Elco displacement cruiser built Bayonne, New Jersey. LOA 33', LWL 30'4", beam 9'4", draft 2'5", cedar deck, mahogany topsides, 1933 Buda 68 hp 6-cylinder engine. Bought in 1973 and restored by the Lazios. Awards: 1978 Best American Built Cruiser & Antique Boat; 1980, 1983 Best Cruiser (Clayton); 1981 Best Antique Cruiser (MCBC); 1983 Best Powerboat (Mystic Rendezvous).

Martin Earle Leggett
ACAJOU 32E7780
Ottawa, Ont.
Previous owner: Robert A. Powell

    1956 Century resorter, LOA 18', beam 6'100", draft 29", built in Michigan of acajou (mahogany), fitted with the original 1956 Gray 135 6-cylinder engine, 244 cu. in.

Martin Earle Leggett
SUNDANCE

    1977 cedar canoe built in Gravenhurst, Ont. by Greavette, on forms, no ribs, ash trim, gut seats, glass skin over 3/16" cedar, LOA 16'.

Tony Lewis
RIOT
Vero Beach, Fla.
Previous owner: *Ted Warner*

1950 Class E service runabout, double-cockpit, racing, by Davis Bros. of Manteo, North Carolina, plywood construction, LOA 17'6", LWL 17', beam 5'6", draft 12", fitted with original 1950 Gray marine Fireball engine, approx. 210 cu. in. Awards: 1987 Classic Boat of the Year (MCBC).

Jim & Tony Lewis
MAVOURNEEN 1298GP
New York & Clayton, NY

1930 yacht tender, built by Camper & Nicholson of Gosport, England, as a tender for J-boats racing in the America Cup races. Carvel-built of mahogany, LOA 50', LWL 48', beam 8', draft 3', fitted with 1987 Pleasure Craft engine, 454 cu. in. Awards: 1988 Best of Show (Biscayne, Florida); 1988 Peoples Choice & Best Antique Launch (MCBC).

J.P. Lewis
YESTERDAY
Clayton, NY
Previous owners: *George C. Boldt, E.J. Noble*
Previous names: *This, June II*

1910 racing launch built by Leyare of Ogdensburg, NY, designed by Charles D. Mower, carvel-built of cedar, LOA 26', LWL 26', beam 4'8", draft 10", fitted with a replacement engine, a 1930 vintage 109 hp Gray. Awards: numerous, including 1985 Historic Boat of the Year (Muskoka) & 1985 Historic Boat of the Year (MCBC).

J.P. Lewis
CORSAIR
Clayton, NY
Previous owners: *Fred C. Hard, J.P. Morgan*

1939 yacht launch designed by Herreshoff and built at Bristol, Rhode Island, carvel-built of teak, fitted with 1987 Pleasure Craft 350 cu. in. engine. Built as starboard launch for J.P. Morgan's *Corsair* IV, never put on board due to World War II. Awards: 1980 Best Launch & People's Choice; 1983 Longest Trailer Haul; 1986 Best Antique Launch (MCBC) and others too numerous to list.

J.P. Lewis
SWIFTWATER

1938 carvel-built custom runabout from Hutchinson Boat Works, Alexandria Bay, NY, LOA 28', LWL 27', beam 7', draft 12", carvel-built mahogany, triple cockpit,. single windshield, fitted with 1950 universal 175 hp engine.

Dave Linkletter
YNYESCRAIG
Gananoque & Manotick, Ont.
Previous owner: *Davey Belfie*

Circa 1920 W.J. Malette launch, LOA 26', beam 6', draft 1', cedar hull, mahogany decks. Built Gananoque, Ont. with 1919 model 20 Kermath 20 hp engine. Davey Belfie worked for owners of Ynyescraig Island in St. Lawrence. Awards: 1980 Best Canadian Boat (Clayton); 1981 Best Launch (MCBC); 1981 Craftsmanship (Clayton); 1983 Professional Craftsmanship (MCBC).

Dave Linkletter
Unnamed 40E442
Lansdowne & Manotick, Ont.
Previous owner: George Morse

1929 Edwin Long carvel-built runabout, redwood seats, oak frames, cyprus hull, mahogany decks. Built Rochester, NY., engine 1941 Sea King outboard 15.2 hp, 25 cu. in., restored 1985. Awards: 1985 Best Boat and Motor Combination (Clayton); 1986 Best Boat and Motor Combination (MCBC).

Chris Lucas
Unnamed 86E2754
Orillia & Rideau Lakes, Ont.

1949-51(?) Shepherd carvel-built runabout LOA 22', LWL 22', beam 7'4", draft 2', mahogany on oak with curved transom. Built Niagara-on-the-Lake, with 1949 Chrysler M27 115 hp 250 cu. in. engine. Boat currently undergoing restoration.

Rod J. Maclean
Unnamed 50E11669
Port Carling, Ont.
Previous owner: Gord Lang

1938 Johnston clinker-built, mahogany inboard runabout, built in Port Carling with Buchanan 6-cylinder Meteor 100 hp engine. Now in storage at Rockport, Ontario, awaiting some hull restoration.

Alan C. Macleod
LEGAL TENDER 64E-599
Leamington & Manotick, Ont.

1953 carvel-built mahogany special sportsman Chris-Craft utility runabout, LOA 17'7", LWL 17', beam 7', draft 1'5", built Algonac, Michigan, with 1953 Chris-Craft KLC 120 hp engine, restored by Millar-Potter, Manotick, Ont., 1985, engine rebuilt 1987. Awards: 1985 & 1988 Best Utility; 1986 Classic Boat of the Year, co-winner (MCBC).

Manotick Ladies Antique Rowing Club
CYRIL
Ottawa, Ont.
Previous owner: Mr. Boyd

Pre-1890 Searle rowing shell, LOA 42', beam 36", draft 6", built in Lambeth, England, of pitch pine, mahogany, ash ribs, and sent to Canada for Mr. Boyd's sons to practise rowing before they went to Oxford. In storage 1916-86. Awards: 1986 Canadian Classic Boat the Year (Clayton); 1986 & 1988 Oldest Boat of the Show; 1986 Historic Boat of the Year; 1987 Longest Water Voyage Self-Propelled (MCBC).

Louis & Michele Martineau
CHIMERE 193082
Ottawa, Ont.
Previous owners: Miron brothers, Montreal; Dr. G. Drouin; Marcel Piche QC, Montreal; Auguste Martineau, Ottawa.
Previous name: Pollywog.

1946 classic Chris-Craft carvel-built mahogany cabin cruiser, LOA 42', LWL 40', beam 12', draft 3'6". Built Algonac, Michigan, fitted with 1977 twin Chrysler engines, each 400 cu. in. Frequently used to entertain dignitaries including Prince Charles and Princess Diana. Awards: 1981 Best Canadian Cruiser (Clayton); 1983 Best Classic Cruiser; 1984 Best Chris-Craft (MCBC).

Ann & Michael Matheson
TRADITION
Miami, Florida
Previous owners: *Bob Mackay; and three before him.*
Previous name: *Dispute III.*

 1929 Chris-Craft Commuter, carvel-built of Honduras mahogany with white pine decks, LOA 38', LWL 37', beam 9'6", draft 3', fitted with 1987 400 hp Wing engine, 454 cu. in. Awards: 1984 Best Chris-Craft Cruiser, Best Antique Cruiser, People's Choice, travelled the farthest distance (MCBC).

Al & Bev McKenney
Unnamed 31E6670
Previous owner: *Bill Moore*

 1942 carvel-built Philippine mahogany deluxe Chris-Craft utility runabout, LOA 18'1", beam 6'4", draft 1'3", Ford engine. Under restoration.

Al & Bev McKenney
OLYVE-ED 3222156
Previous owners: *Olyve & Edward McKenney*

 Circa 1930 Dowsett clinker-built cedar lap power skiff, LOA 21'6", beam 4', draft 2'6". Built Portland, Ont. with 1930(?) St. Lawrence 2-cylinder 6-8 hp inboard engine. Originally bought by Mr. Ed McKenney and kept in the family. Awards: 1986 Best Power Skiff (Clayton).

Robert Merkley
MARION 32E1543
Ottawa, Ont.
Previous owner: *Cam Merkley.*

 1956 carvel-built mahogany Shepherd-decked runabout, LOA 18', LWL 15'6", beam 6'4", draft 18". Built Niagara-on-the-Lake, with 1956 Chrysler Royal Crown 135 hp engine. Bought with savings for living-room furniture, hence mother's name, *Marion*. Awards: 1977 Best Shepherd (MCBC).

C. Howard Metcalfe
SYRO
Ottawa, Ont.
Previous owner: *Howard Rees*

 1946 Midland carvel-built cedar-and-white-oak bridge deck cruiser, LOA 30', LWL 28'5", beam 10', draft 3'. Designed by Eldridge McInnis Inc. and built at Midland Boat Works. Fitted with 1963 Chrysler ACE 110 hp engine.

James Millar
Unnamed

 1937 clinker-built mahogany Dowsett runabout, LOA 18', beam 4', draft 10", built in Portland, Ont., with 1937 or pre-1937 St. Lawrence engine.

John R. Millar
ACE
Manotick, Ont.
Previous owners: *Charles Howe, H.E. Howe*

 1902 Peterborough V-deck sailing canoe, shiplap strip, LOA 16', beam 32", copper nail and brass screw fastenings, cedar, elm and walnut wood.

John R. Millar
ALOHA
Manotick, Ont.

 1932 Peterborough Speedster outboard runabout, LOA 13', beam 5', shiplap strip of cedar and oak, fitted with 1939 Evinrude.

John R. Millar
BURLEIGH
Manotick, Ont.
Previous owner: *Mrs. Gordon Howe*

 1930 Peterborough rowing skiff, LOA 16', beam 3'6", shiplap strip with original copper nail and brass screw fastenings, elm, cedar and oak wood.

John R. Millar
COMET
Manotick, Ont.
> 1937 Peterborough Comet inboard runabout, LOA 16'6", beam 6', draft 18", carvel-built of mahogany and oak, fitted with 1937 Buchanan engine.

John R. Millar
TRAVELLER
Manotick, Ont.
Previous owner: David Bartlett
> 1922 Peterborough runabout, gasoline powered, LWL 18', beam 5', shiplap strip planking with copper nail, cedar, oak and mahogany wood.

Peter Milne
EVENTIDE RAMBLER
Smiths Falls, Ont.
Previous owners: J.P. Elwood, W. Jones
> 1953 cedar boat with outboard engine, possibly a Peterborough, LOA 16'.

Peter Milne
Unnamed
> Cedar boat, date not known, possibly a Peterborough, LOA 14'.

Lise & Jean-Francois Milotte
PANACEA 32E29202
Ottawa & Manotick, Ont.
Previous owners: Dr. Stuart J. Millar, Commodore A.T. Arnott
> 1967 Pacemaker motor yacht, carvel-built of mahogany-on-oak frames, LOA 39'10", LWL 37' (approx.), beam 14'6", draft 3'6". Designed by C.P. Leek & Sons Inc., built Egg Harbour, New Jersey, with twin Pacemaker 320 hp GM engines, fully equipped with modern navigational aids. Awards: 1985 Best Classic Cruiser; 1986 Contemporary Classic Cruiser (MCBC).

Bill, Jane & Elizabeth Moore
LIZA JANE
Portland, Ont.
Previous owners: Gerry Purcell, Tom Purcell
> 1945 Dowsett rowing skiff designed and built by Will Dowsett in Portland. Original fittings.

Bill, Jane & Elizabeth Moore
RIDEAU PASSAGE
Portland, Ont.
Previous owners: Tom Purcell, Dan Slack, May family.
> 1915 Nichol motor launch, LOA 23'6", beam 4', 1929 4-cylinder gas Kermath engine. Built in Smiths Falls by Davy Nichol using cedar, oak, cherry and butternut woods, original finishings, chrome fastenings, mahogany transom edge-railed flush planking, flat bottom, rounding to chine, open white river launch with long butternut deck. Awards: 1982 Best Boat on the Rideau Lakes; 1983 Best Historic Runabout (MCBC).

Bill, Jane & Elizabeth Moore
EL TORO
Portland, Ont.

    1954 Greavette utility runabout, LOA 20'7", draft 2', 1954 Crown flathead 6, gas engine, carved-mahogany transom, double bottom, original upholstery fittings and chrome fastenings. Awards: 1986 Longest Water Voyage Self Propelled (MCBC).

Brian & Olive Payne
Unnamed

    1973 voyageur cedar-strip canvas-covered canoe, LOA 18'. Built by Chestnut, New Brunswick.

Frank Phelan
LILLIAN T. II 6E296
Brockville & Manotick, Ont.
Previous owners: Fleishmann family, Layng family, John Johnston.
Previous name: Y-Knaut

    1924 carvel-built launch, mahogany deck, cedar sides and bottom. Built Brockville, fitted with 1947 Kermath 6-cylinder Sea Prince engine, a Gilbert but indentical to the 1924 Peterborough autocraft. Awards: 1977 Best Canadian Runabout (MCBC).

Jim & Diane Phillips
Unnamed

    Circa 1910 Peterborough carvel-built double-ended canoe, cedar on oak, LOA 16', given to Jim Phillips' father in 1913. Now in storage awaiting stripping and refinishing.

Jim & Diane Phillips
Unnamed

    1955(?) Shepherd carvel-built mahogany double-cockpit runabout, LOA 22', beam 6'10". Built Niagara-on-the-Lake, with 1955 Chrysler M45 V-drive marine engine mounted in stern. Under restoration in New Brunswick.

Doug & Nancy Porter
RAZZ MA TAZZ 15E1032
Kingston & Portland, Ont.
Previous owners: Peter & Marian Burchell, Gord Taber

    1955 Shepherd carvel-built mahogany runabout, built Niagara-on-the-Lake, with Chrysler marine engine, LOA 22', LWL 21', beam 7'6", draft 2'. Awards: 1984 Best Boat on the Rideau Lakes; 1984 & 1986 Classic Boat of the Year; 1986 Best Canadian Built Boat; 1988 Best Engine Compartment (MCBC).

James C. Potter
ARAWAN 74E140
Smiths Falls & Portland, Ont.
Previous owner: Wendell Hughes

    1929 carvel-built Dowsett displacement launch, cedar hull on white oak frames. Honduras mahogany decks, LOA, 29', beam 5'9", draft 17", built Portland, Ont., with St. Lawrence model FT engine, now fitted with 1923 Scripps F4 64 hp engine. In storage at present. Awards: 1976 Best Canadian Boat of the Year – Runabout (MCBC); 1976 Best Dowsett (MCBC); 1977 Best Canadian Launch (MCBC); 1979 Best Launch (MCBC).

James C. Potter
RIOT II 32E5256
Ottawa & Manotick, Ont.
Previous owners: Mr. Potter, Mr. Gamble, Bill Watson

    1940-41 E.A. Andress mahogany-on-oak split-cockpit runabout, LOA 18', beam 5'11", draft 16", one of perhaps two hard-chine boats built by Andress in Rockport, Ont.

James C. Potter
JIM'S JAM 74E5179
Smiths Falls & Portland, Ont.

    1941 Chris-Craft runabout, carvel-built, LOA 22', beam 5'11", fitted with 1941 Chris-Craft Model M engine, 339 cu. in. displacement. Award: 1983 Best Utility (MCBC).

Brian E. Pye
EMPRESS FLAGSHIP EXPRESS 50E40053
Rockport & Hurst Marina, Ont.
Previous owners: P.M. Kelly, Frank Keeler
Previous names: Special "K", Windrift

    1962 Owens hardtop cruiser, carvel-built mahogany with teak and nautolex decks, LOA 30', beam 11', draft 3', fitted with 4M Flagship twin engines, 185 hp.

Wayne & Elsie Read
MICHELLE
Belleville, Bay of Quinte, Hayward Long Reach, Ont.
Previous owners: John B. Horner, Michael Machibroda

    1956 Greavette utility runabout, clinker-built of mahogany, oak and fir plywood, LOA 20'6", beam 8'2", draft 2', fitted with original 1956 Ford V8 engine, 292 cu. in. Award: 1985 Craftsmanship (MCBC).

John D. Richards
LYNDA IV 193652
Ottawa & Poonamalie, Ont.

    1939 Chris-Craft sedan cruiser, hull no. 33546, carvel-built in Algonac, Michigan of mahogany, LOA 33', LWL 31', beam 12'2", draft 2'6", fitted with twin Chris-Craft 6-cylinder Hercules engines (not the originals, which were 4-cylinder).

Adrian N. Richmond
MISS LITTLEHAMPTON
Previous owner: Stuart McEwen
Previous name: FCK

    Circa 1950 Burleigh model rowing skiff by Peterborough Canoe, carvel-built of cedar-strip planking with ash ribs, oak keel and pine seats, LOA 16'2", LWL 16', beam 3'8½", draft 8", fitted with 1926 Johnson 1.5 hp outboard, a ½"-wide walnut strip 3" below the top of the gunwhale.

John Ritchie
GLENELEN
Bracebridge & Manotick, Ont.
Previous owners: Glen Bailey, Douglas Bailey

    1953 carvel-built Peterborough cedar-strip canoe, white cedar and white oak planking on white oak and ash framing, LOA 16', LWL 15'6", beam 5'6", built Peterborough, fitted with 1958 Evinrude 35 hp Lark outboard. Restored 1984 by Millar-Potter Boat Works. Awards: 1988 Best Outboard & Boat Combination (MCBC).

Vicki & John Ritchie
SPINDRIFT 50E2659
Toronto & Manotick, Ont.
Previous owners: David P. Rodgers, Sam Rodgers, Alf Sawyer, Louis Ketchell, Rev. Carl Farmer, Clement LaChance, Joseph LaChance, Bob Perry

    1927 Ditchburn carvel-built launch, yellow cedar or cypress planking, spruce, white oak and pine framing, Honduras mahogany decking, LOA 23', LWL 22', beam 6'6", draft 2'6", built Gravenhurst, fitted with 1947 Gray 4-cylinder 75 hp engine. Restored 1986 by Millar-Potter Boat Works.

John Ritchie
Unnamed
Manotick, Ont.

    Circa 1940 Peterborough canoe, cedar planking on cedar-and-white-ash framing, canvas-covered, LOA 16', built in Peterborough.

David & Dinah Scholfield
M'LORA 50E9692
Toronto & Manotick, Ont.
Previous owners: M. Simonds, J. Campbell
Previous name: Truant

    1949 Grew Admiral utility, clinker-built of mahogany on oak frames, LOA 24'6", LWL 24', beam 8'6", draft 33", fitted with standard 1950 Buchanan Comet ML engine, 335 cu. in. Has an unusual history of disasters. Awards: 1987 Best Utility; 1988 Classic Boat of the Year (MCBC).

Carol Simpson & Doug Williams
THE LAUNCH
Whitney, Ont.
Previous owners: R. Geary & Margaret Simpson, B. Roy & Irene Simpson.

    1910 Chestnut motorized canoe built of ash and oak, double planking, LOA 20', beam 5', fitted with circa 1910 St. Lawrence Engine Co. 1-cylinder, 1½ hp engine, later bored at 2 hp. Awards: 1985 Best Skiff, Powered (MCBC).

Dave Sinclair
LA VAGABONDE 170146
Ottawa, Ont.
Previous owners: Ken Narraway, Donald Smith & Arthur Garland, James Redick, Dennis Olliver, John Alexander, Fran Racine
Previous names: Jan Mar, Lady Lea

    1933 carvel-built cruiser by Ernest Therrien of Tetreaultville (Montreal), Quebec. The ribs are white oak, the planks white cedar, and the superstructure mahogany. LOA 35'5", beam 8', draft 30", fitted with a Perkins of Peterborough (England) diesel engine with 305 cu. in. displacement. The engine probably dates from the 1930s. Awards: 1979 People's Choice (MCBC).

John & Francis Suderman
FRAN JAC 51E3117
Trenton, Ont.
Previous owners: Cuttle Marine Gananoque, John R. Mason

    1957 carvel-built mahogany Shepherd, LOA 22', LWL 20', beam 7'4", draft 25", with original Chrysler 265 cu. in. in M475 engine, block rebuilt.

Ron Tackaberry
TACK'S TOY 40E2354
Lansdowne & Charleston Lake, Ont.
Previous name: Sawn Wood II

> 1942 carvel-built mahogany Chris-Craft deluxe utility runabout, LOA 22', beam 7'3", with original Chris-Craft 320.4 cu. in. engine. Built in Algonac, Michigan.

Don & Marlene Thomas
KON TIKI-TOO 32E9533
Ottawa & Portland, Ont.
Previous owner: Christopher T. Thomas

> 1953 carvel-built mahogany Shepherd runabout with original Chrysler Crown 135 hp engine, built Niagara-on-the-Lake, LOA 22', LWL 21', beam 7'8", draft 1'9". Awards: 1979 & 1982 Classic Boat of the Year; 1982, 1986 & 1988 Classic Runabout; 1983 Best Canadian Built Boat; 1985 Best Classic Runabout & Best Boat on the Rideau Lake (MCBC); 1984 Best Shepherd & Best Canadian Built Boat (Can-Am Gananoque); 1982 Best Shepherd & Best Cosmetic Overall (Toronto Chapter ACBS).

Marlene & Don Thomas
LADY GILBERT 6E1
Brockville & Portland, Ont.

> Gilbert launch, carvel-built about 1920 of mahogany-on-oak ribs, LOA 24', beam 5'4", draft 2', with 95% original fittings and a 1947 Kermath 80 hp engine. Awards: 1987 Best Antique Launch & People's Choice (MCBC); 1988 Best Launch (Waterdays Antique and Classic Boat Show, Biscayne Bay, Fla.); 1988 People's Choice (Mt. Dora, Fla.)

A.S. Thompson
WOODWORM 69E1815
Pembroke, Ont.
Previous owner: J.C. Jones

> 1962 Industrial Shipping mahogany ply outboard built by J.C. Jones of Deep River, LOA 16', LWL 15', beam 6', draft 15", fitted with 1959 Mercury Mk 35A 35 hp outboard.

Claude Vickers
ROAM II 32E2573
Ottawa & Kars, Ont.

> 1958 Industrial Shipping moulded plywood outboard runabout with aircraft birch hull, fir plywood seats, mahogany plywood decking, white oak stringers and supports. LOA 15'4", LWL 13', beam 5'8", draft 8" (21' with motor down). Built by Richard and Claude Vickers and fitted with 1963 65 hp 4-cylinder Kiekhaefer Mercury outboard.

William Walker
ALEGRIA 183711
Dartmouth, England & Kingston, Ont.
Previous owners: David R. Walker, Richard Harley Cloudesley King, Arthur Percy Robert, Jean Alethia Violet Canfor.

> 1914 Gaff topsail cutter, carvel-built of pitch pine on oak by W. Frazier & Son of Mevagissey, Cornwall, England. LOA 23' (30' with bowsprit), LWL 23', beam 7'2", draft 5'6", fitted with 1948 Stuart Turner 8 hp engine.

William Walker
DAN
Kingston, Ont.
Previous owner: David Minnes
   1930s vintage clinker-built cat-rigged dinghy, white cedar on oak, LOA 14', with centreboard and midships thwart. Designed and built by George Ackroyd of Toronto. In extended refit.

William Walker
Unnamed
Previous owners: Jenny & Norman Dale
   Motorized rowing skiff of uncertain vintage, 1-cylinder make-and-break engine, fuel tank under bow deck, steering by quadrant on transom-hung rudder.

Byron & Dusty Woods
DIXIE BELLE 32E14182
Ottawa & Portland, Ont.
   1929 carvel-built Colonial BW displacement cruiser, white cedar on oak with rumbarrel mahogany transom, LOA 26', beam 8', draft 2'6", built May Harbour, New Jersey, fitted with 1948 K.L. Hercules 105 hp engine.

Ian Wyllie
SURF SONG
Ottawa, Ont.
Previous owners: Alan Lamport; William Teron; Keith Magee; Karl Hamblin
Previous name: Ja Su Jr.
   1954 Shepherd model 110 runabout mahogany on oak, LOA 22', LWL 21'9", beam 7'4", draft 2'. Built Niagara-on-the-Lake and fitted with 1954 Chrysler Marine hemi V-drive hydraulic engine.

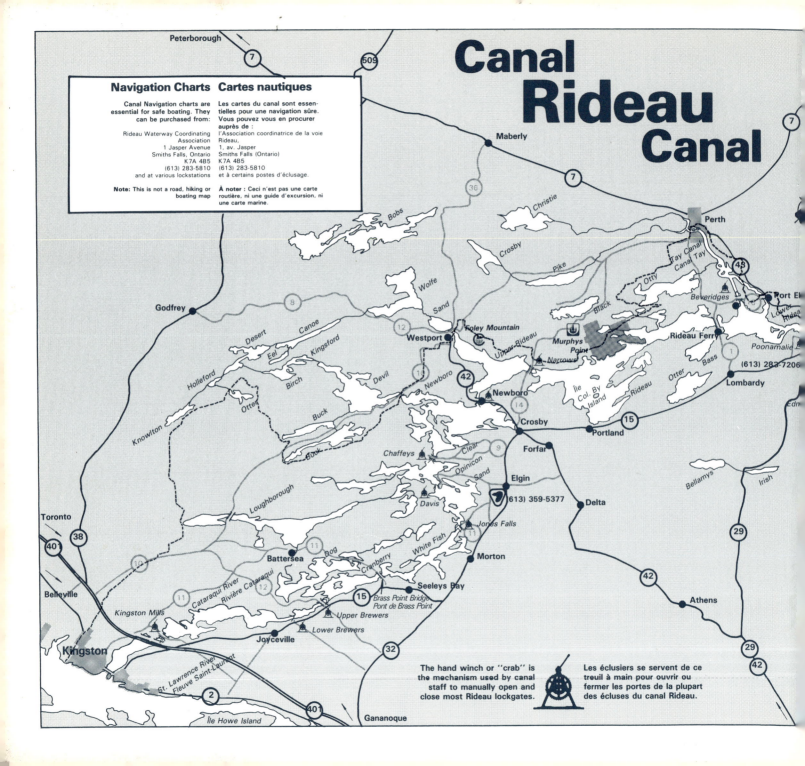